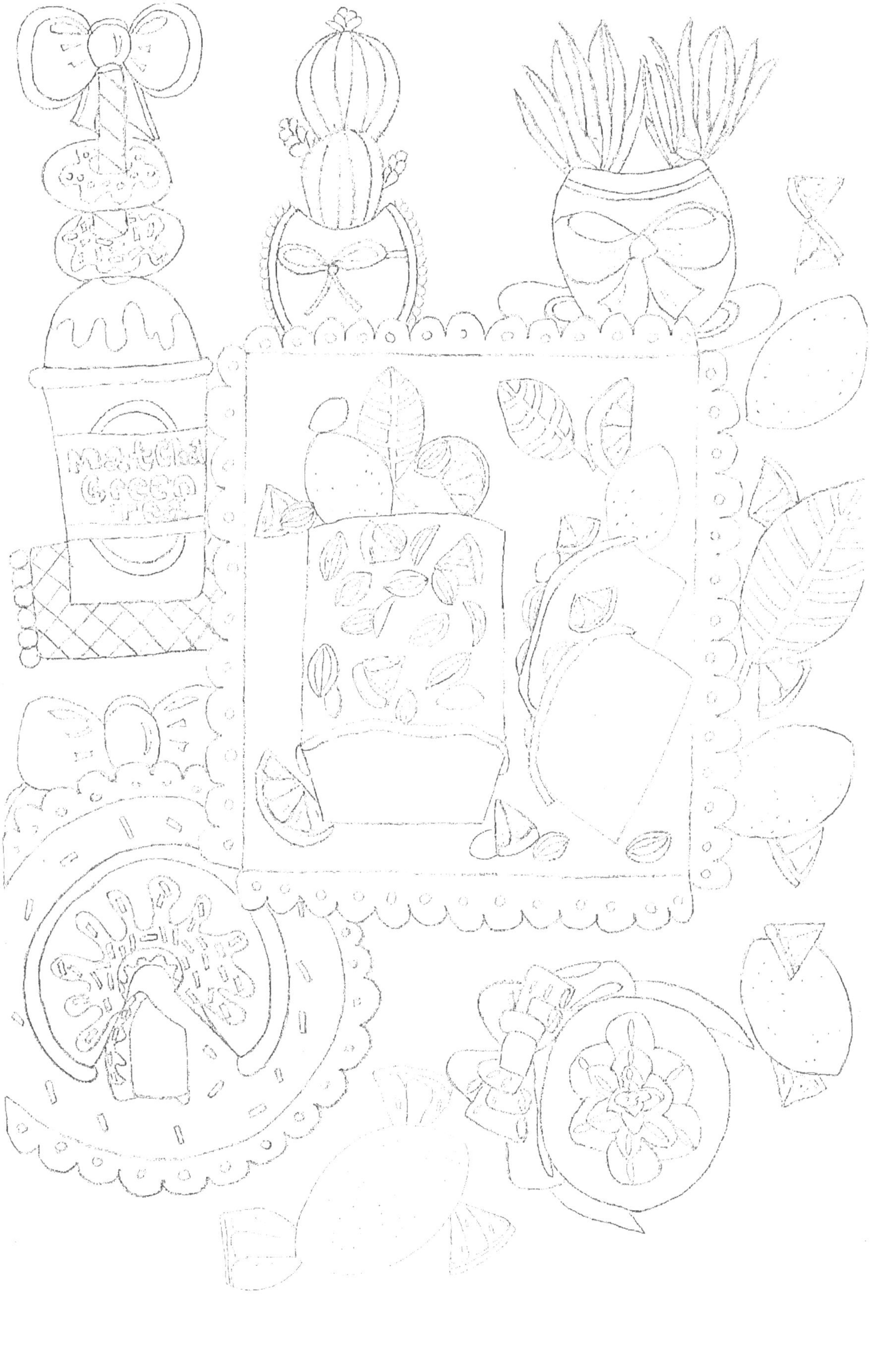
matcha
green
tea

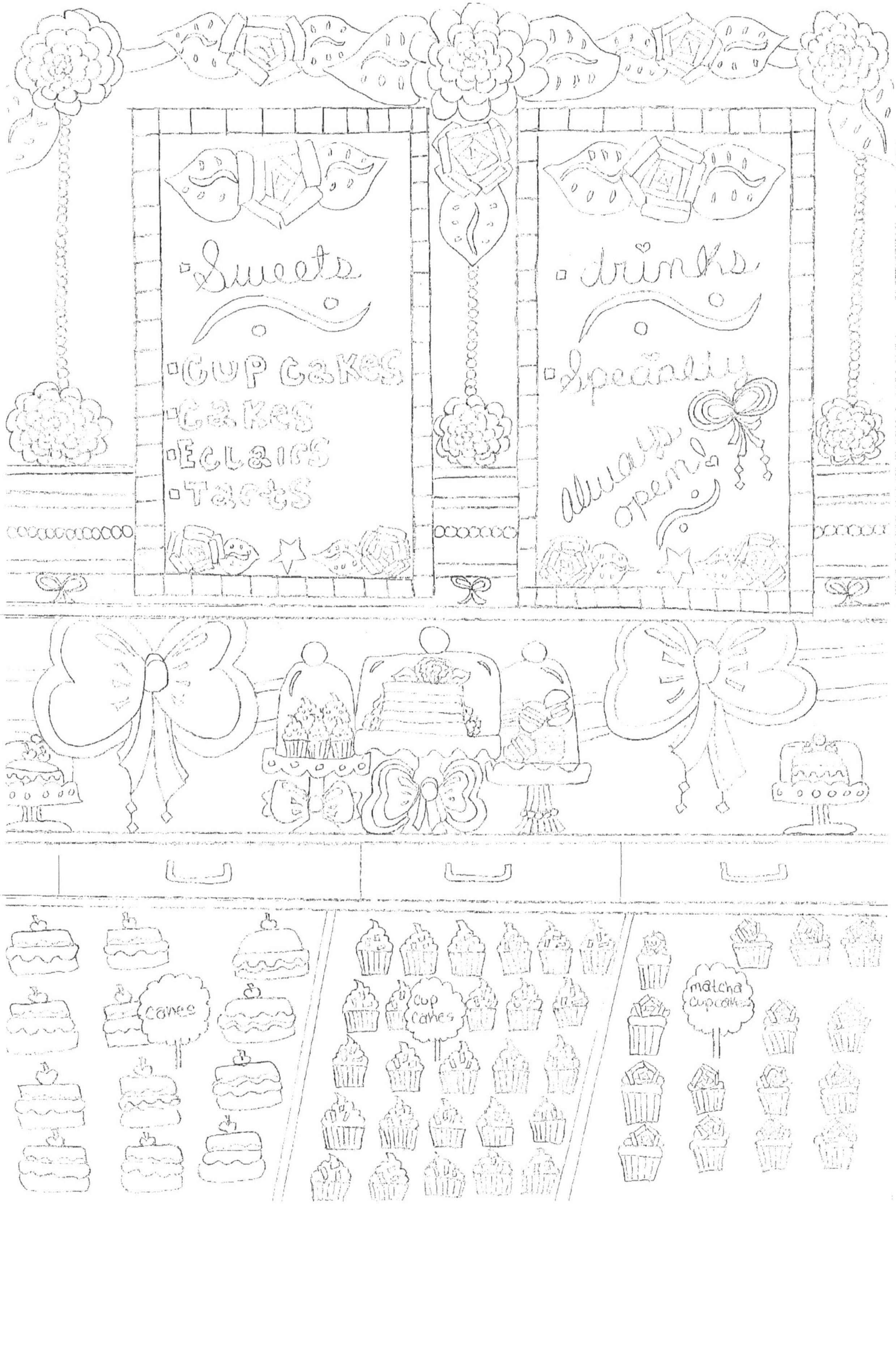
Sweets
Cup cakes
Cakes
Eclairs
Tarts
drinks
Specialty
always open!
cakes
cup cakes
matcha cupcakes

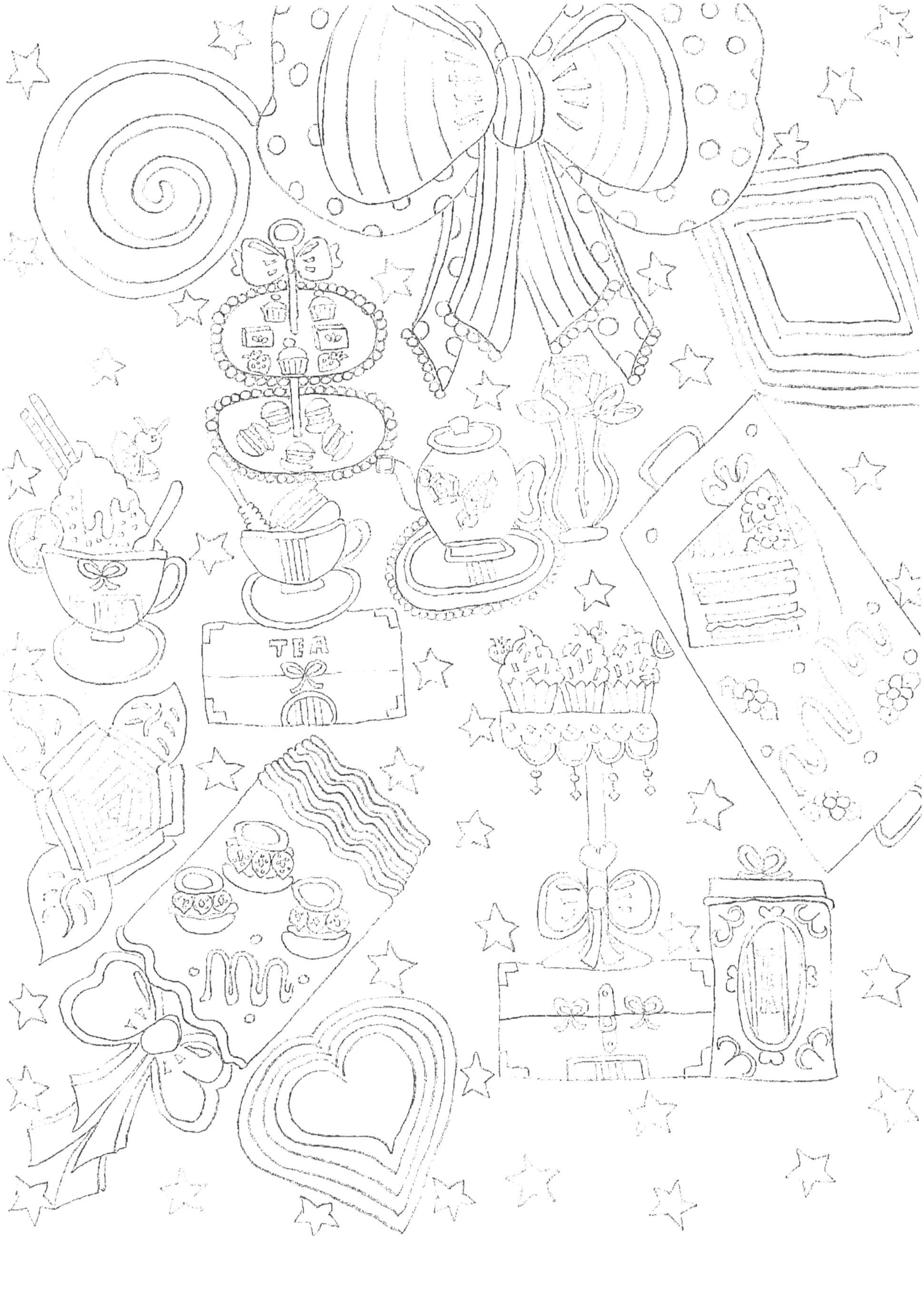
TEA

TEA
TEA
TEA
ALMOND MILK
COCONUT MILK
CASHEW MILK
CREAM
SOY MILK

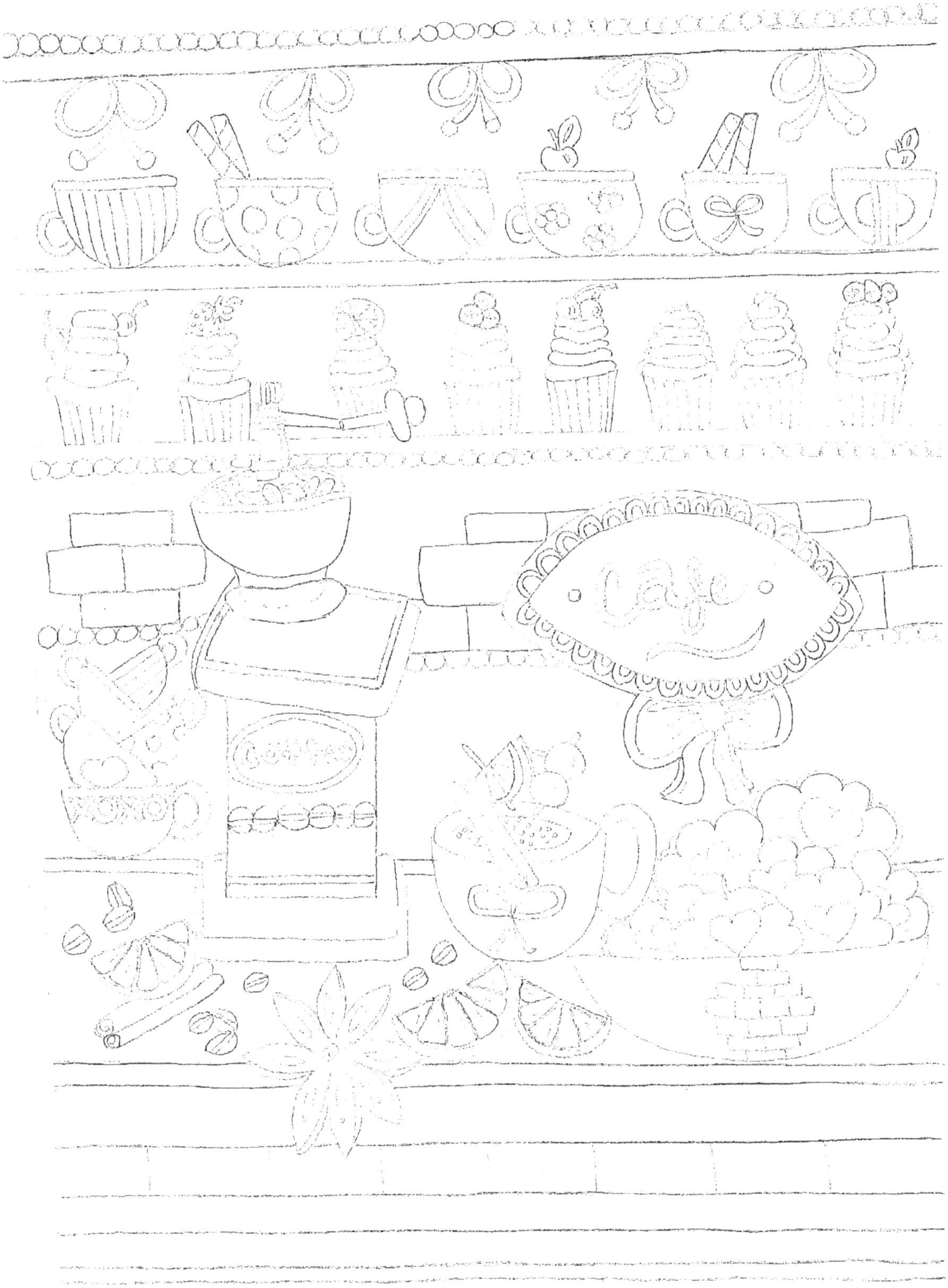
Cafe
Coffee
XOXO

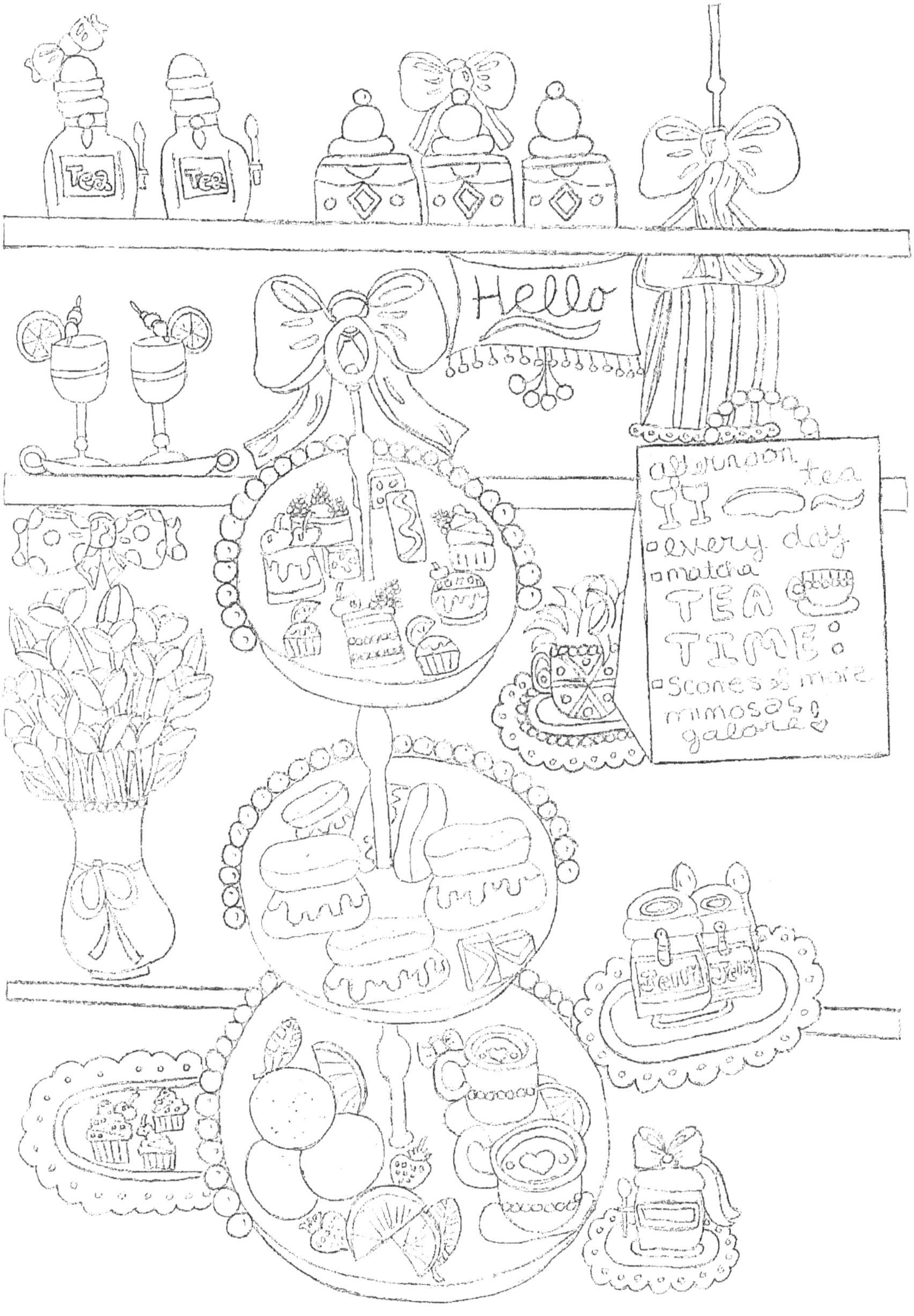
Tea
Tea
Hello
afternoon tea
every day
matcha
TEA TIME!
scones & more
mimosas galore

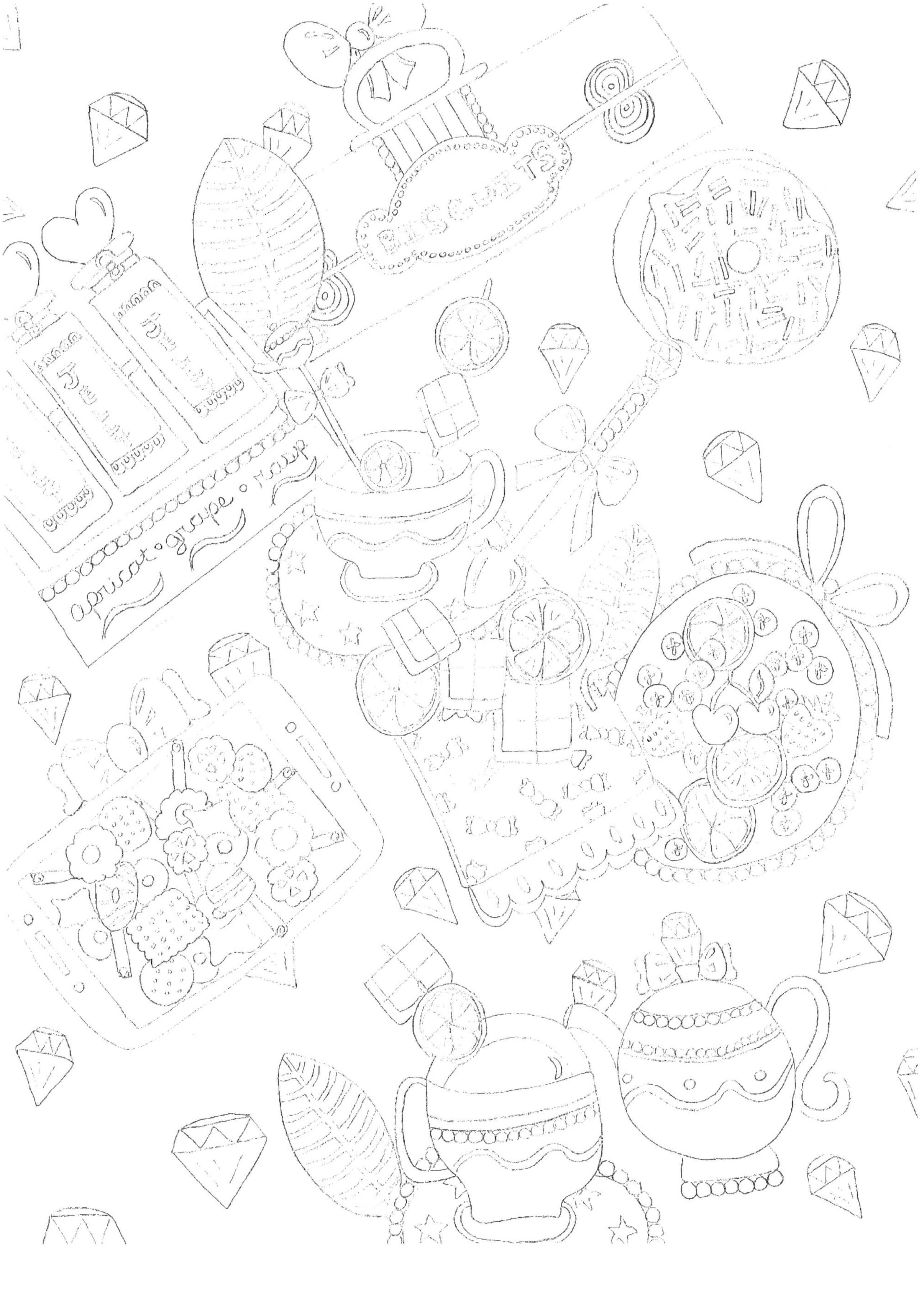
BISCUITS
apricot · grape · mango

The Tea Garden

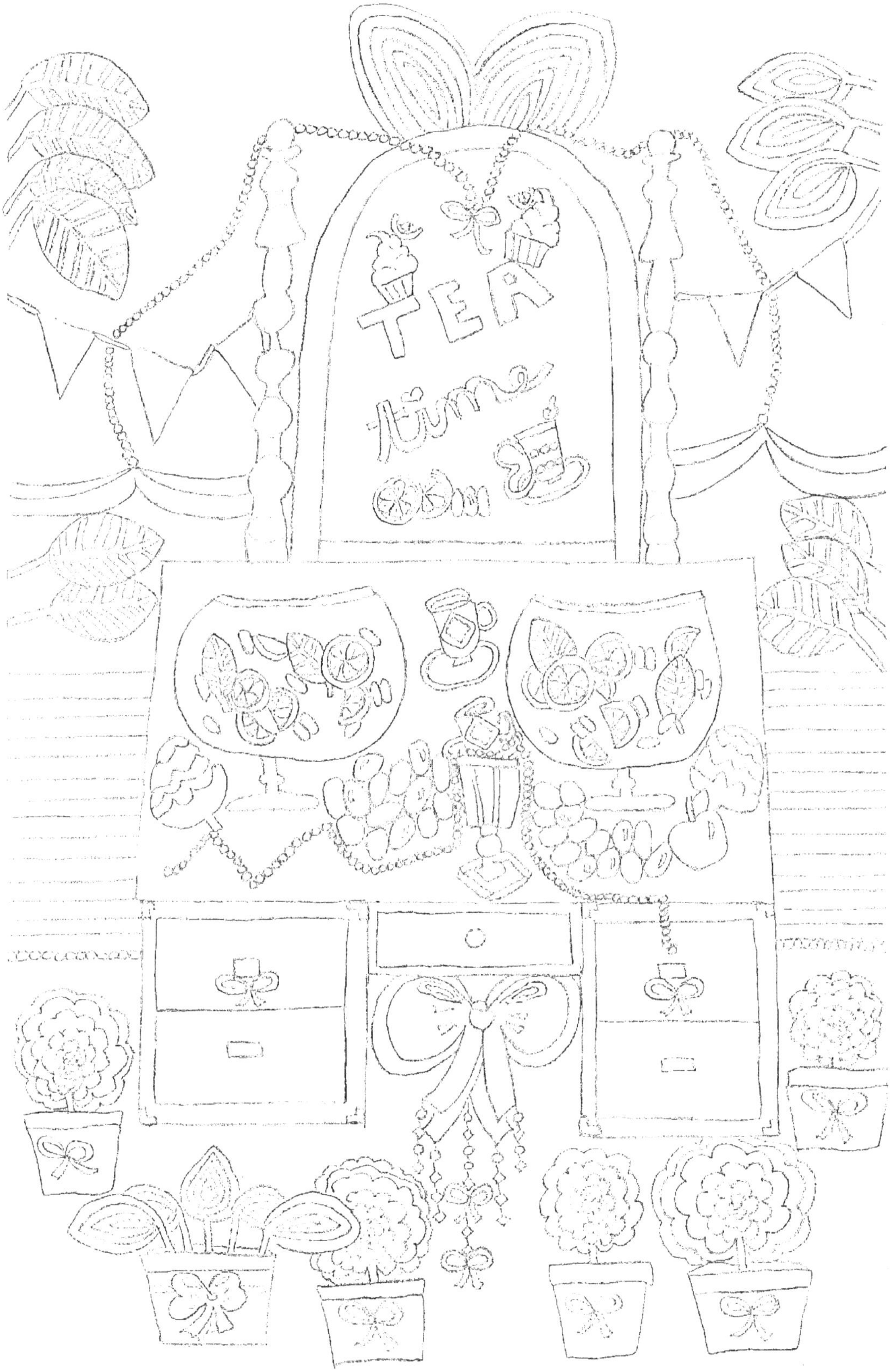
TEA time

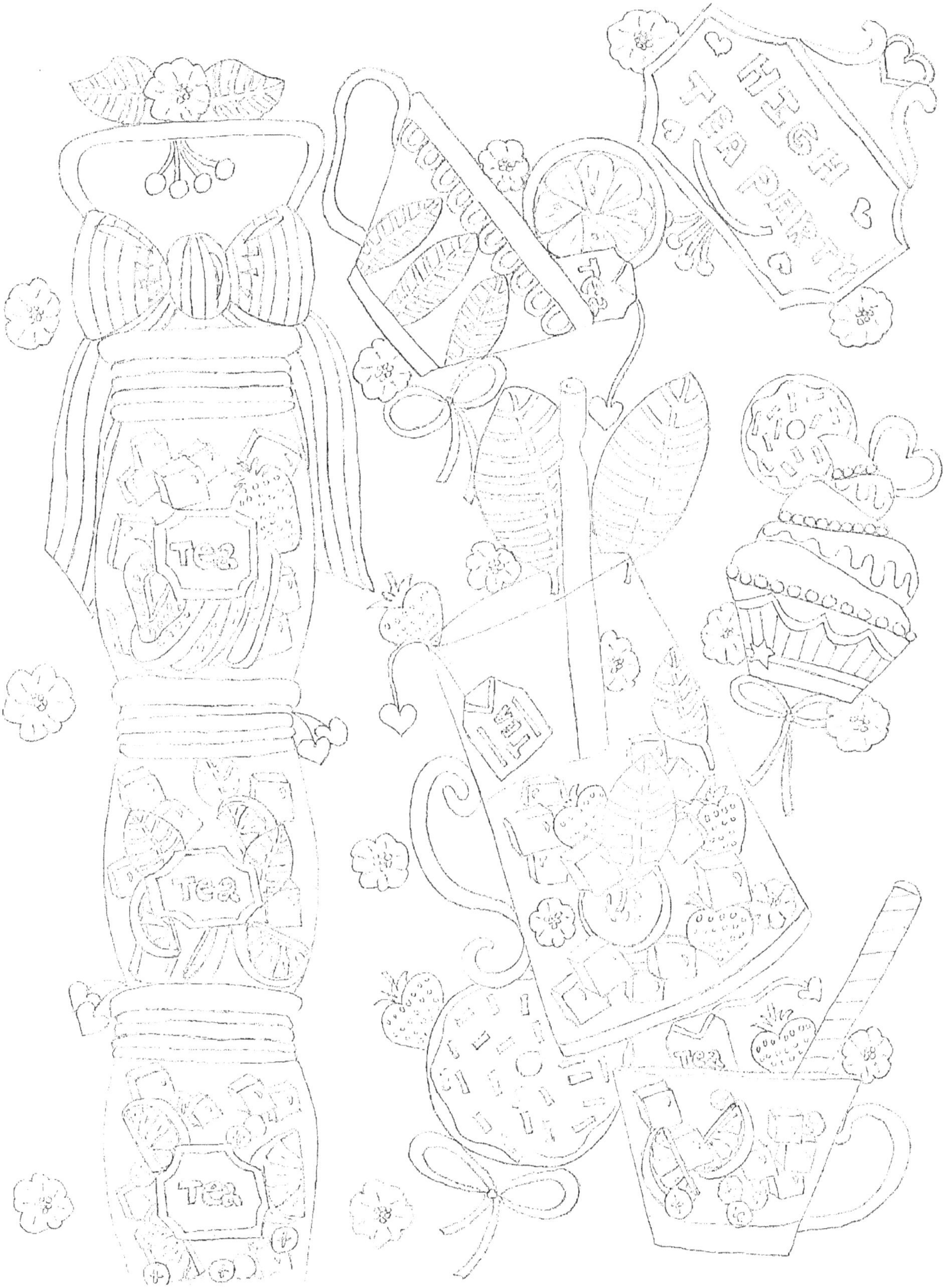
HIGH TEA PARTY
Tea
Tea
Tea
Tea
Tea
Tea
Tea

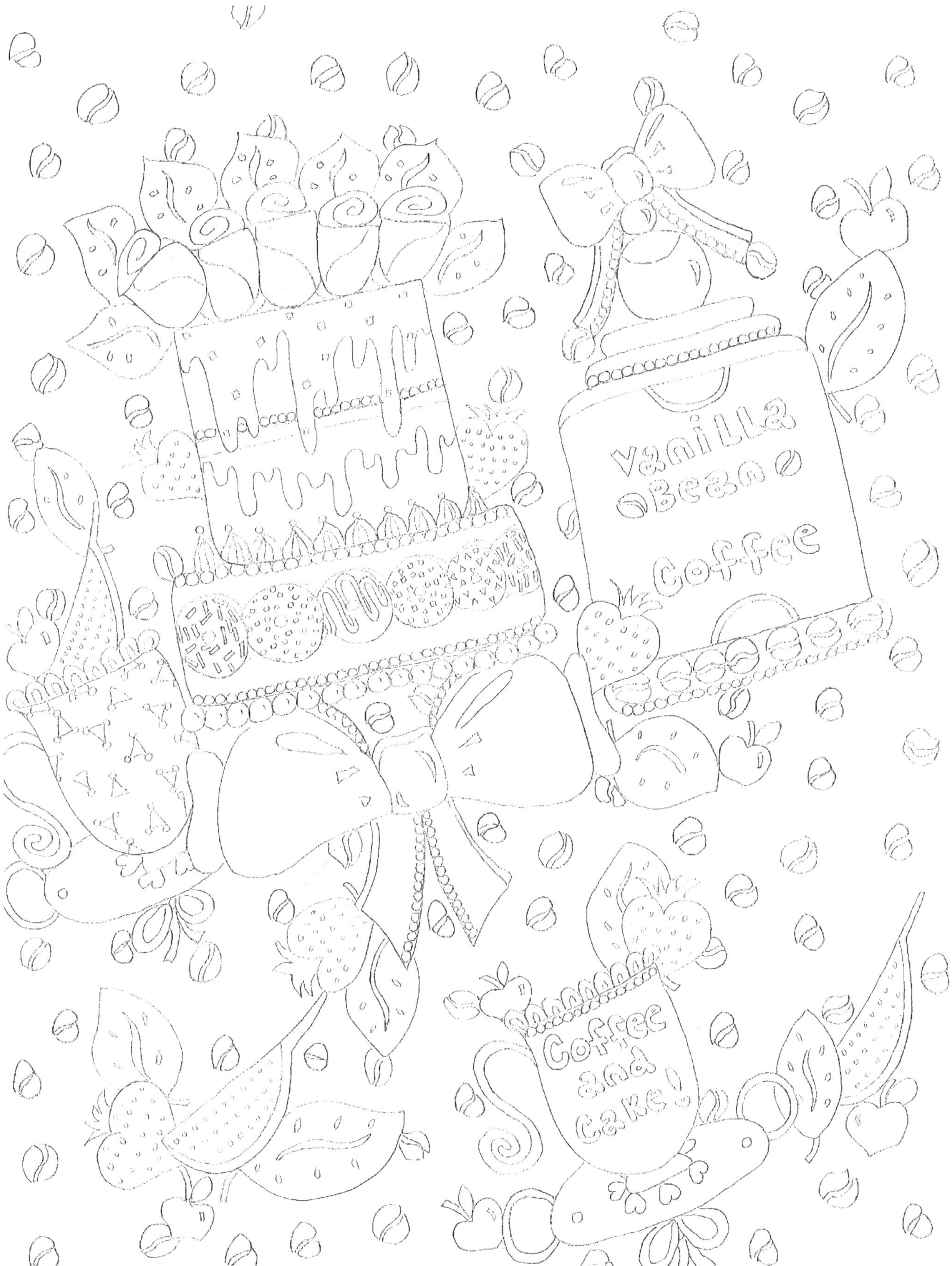
Vanilla Bean Coffee
Coffee and Cake!

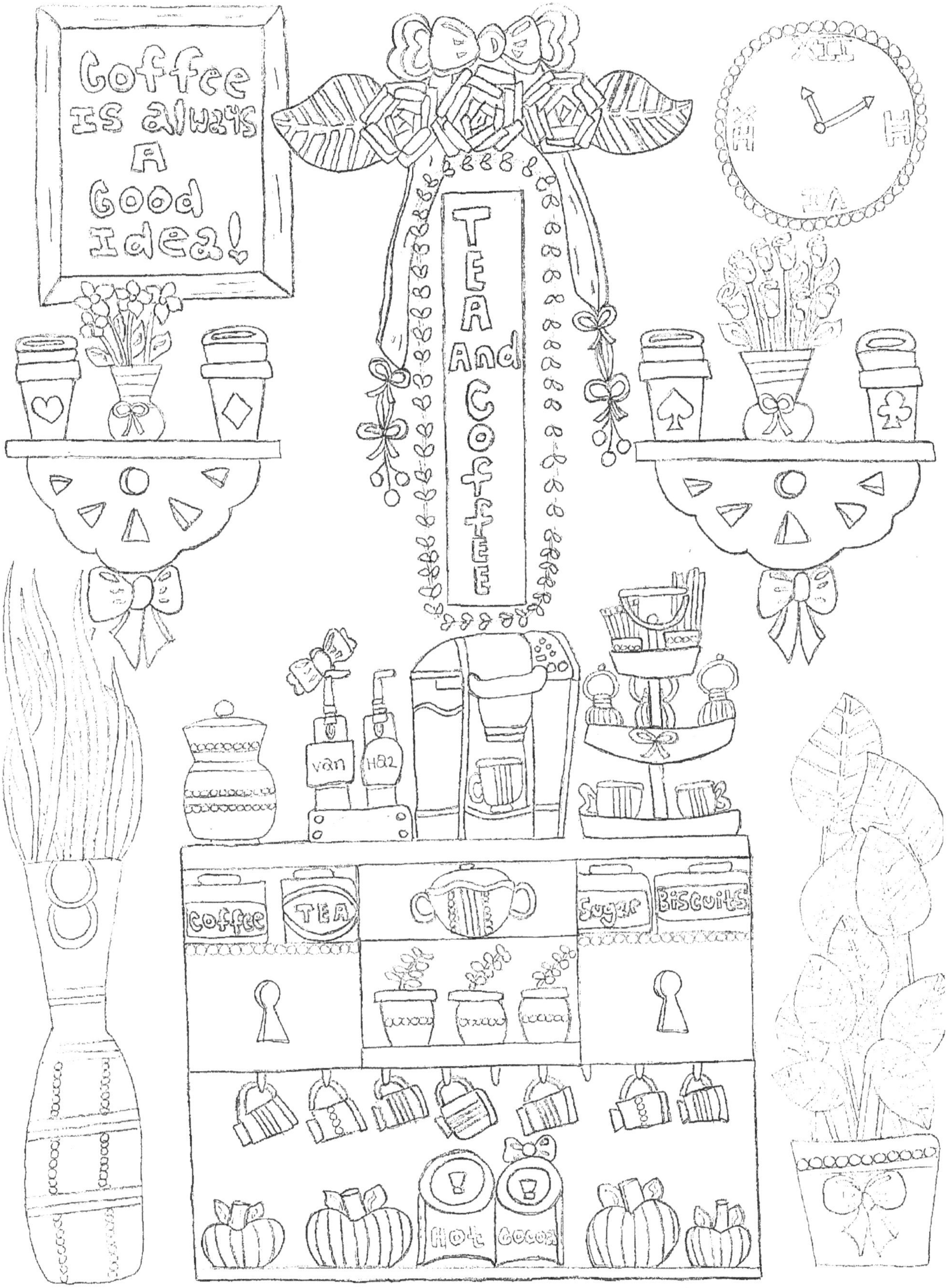
Coffee is always a Good idea!
TEA And Coffee
van
Haz
coffee
TEA
Sugar
Biscuits
Hot Cocoa

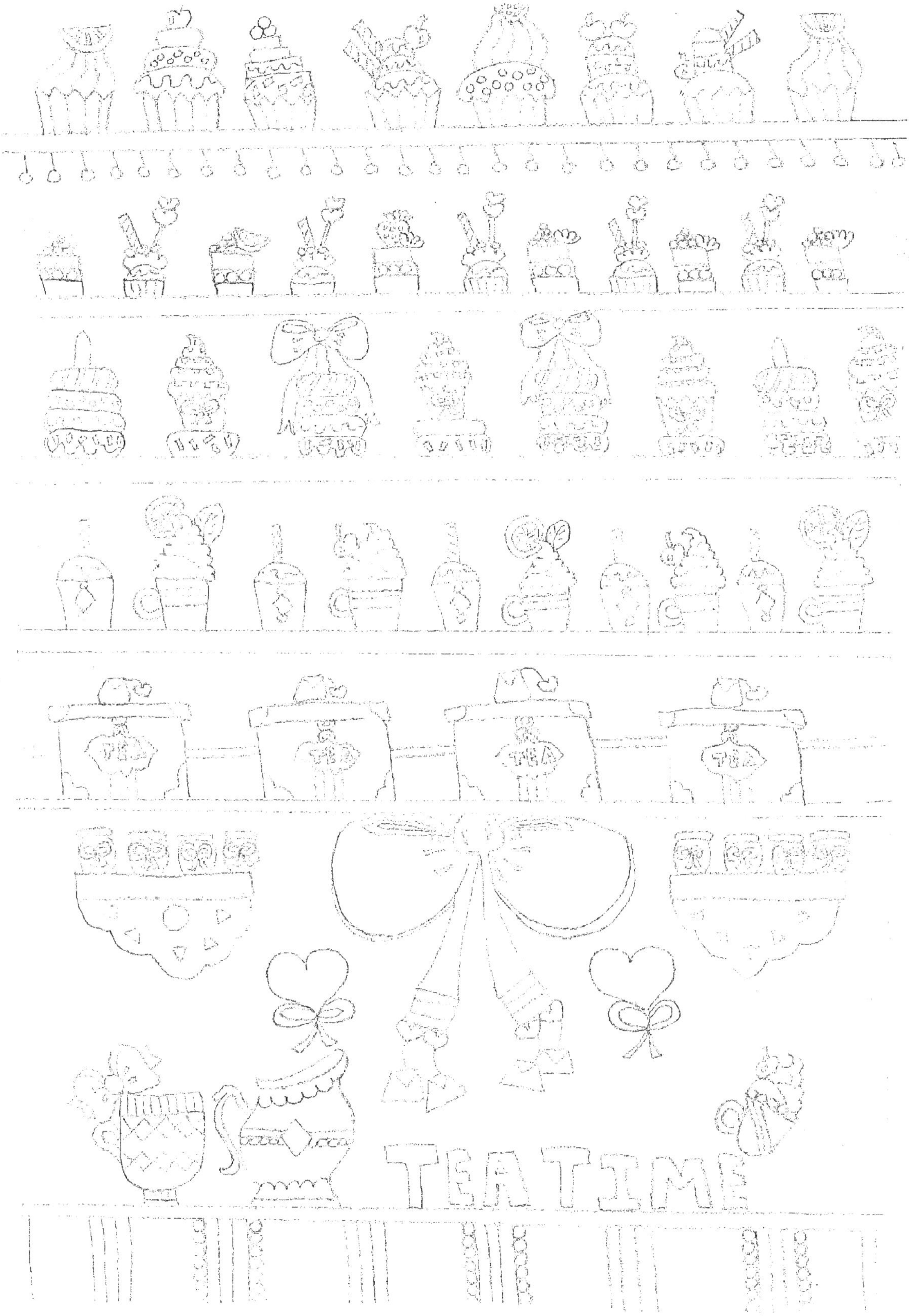
TEA TIME

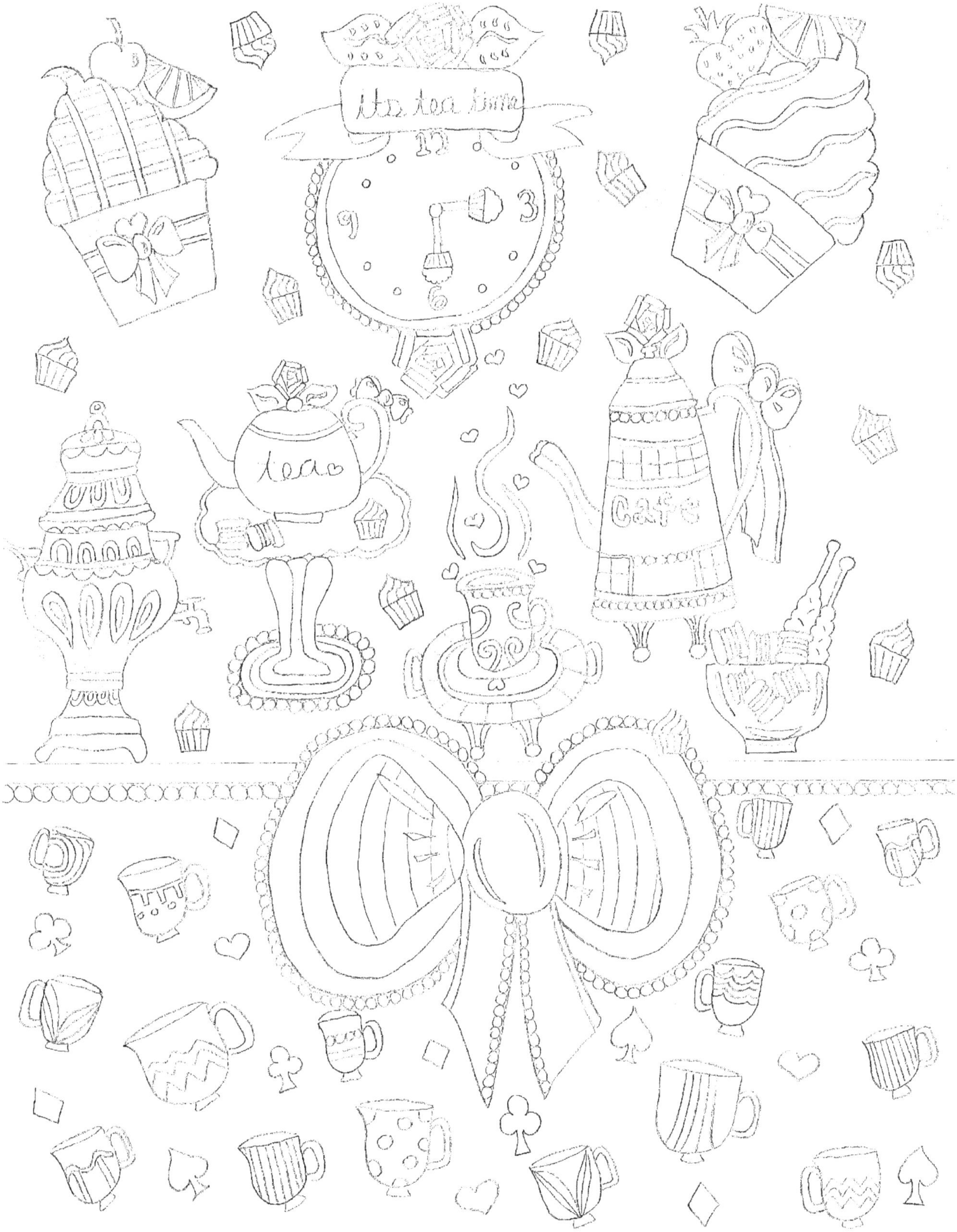
Its tea time
tea
cafe

TEA
COFFEE

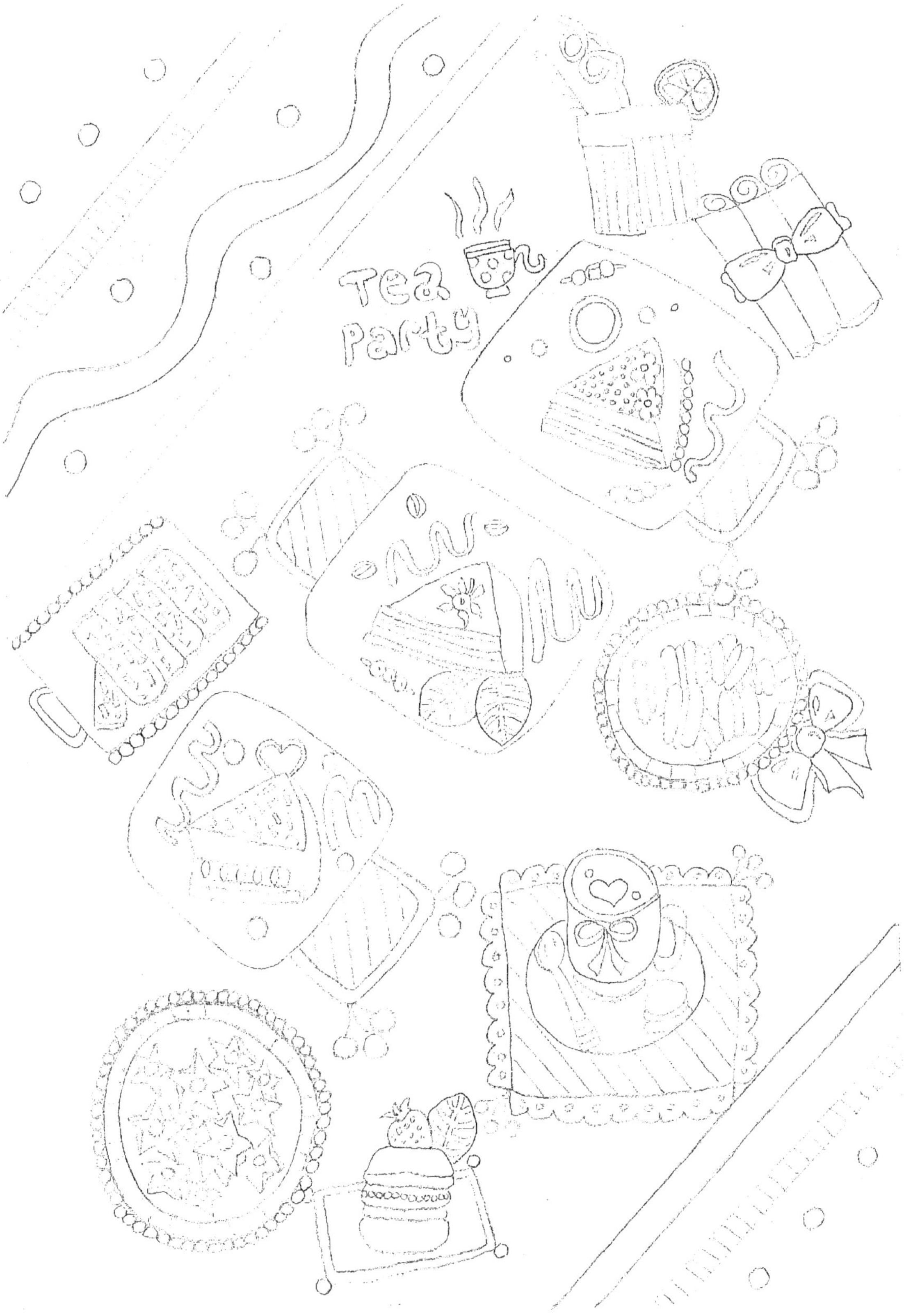
Tea
Party

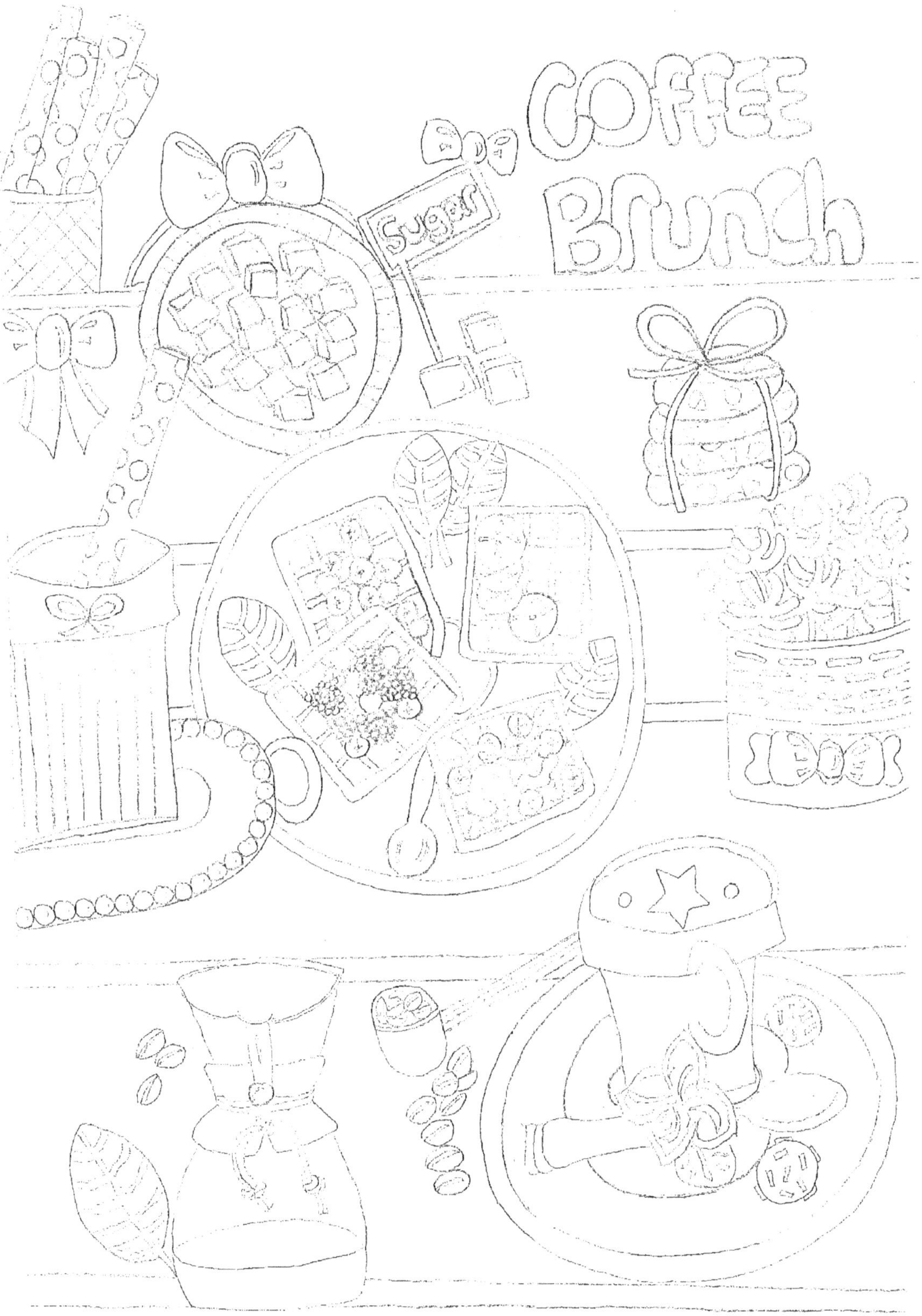
COFFEE
Brunch
Sugar

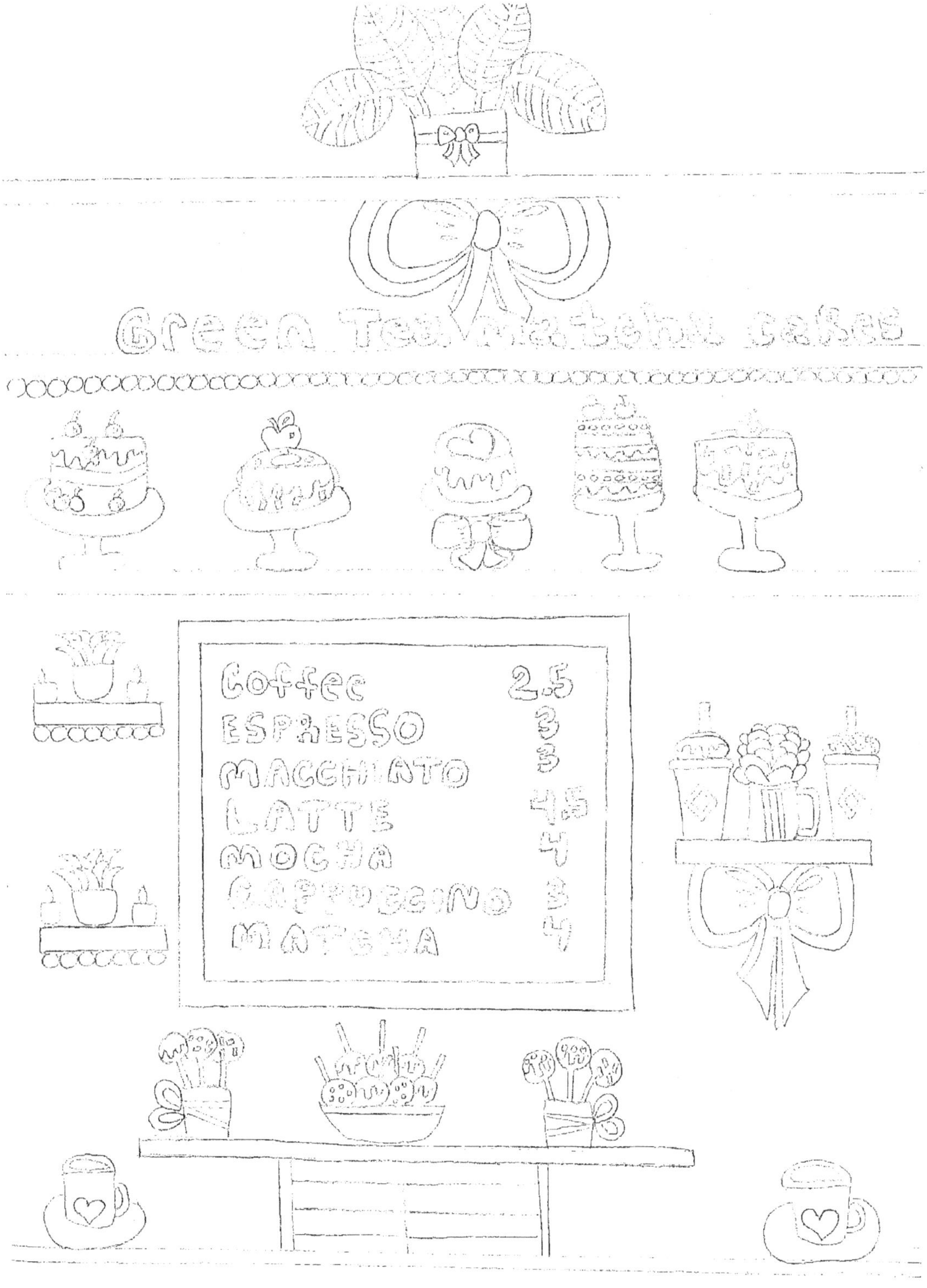

Green Tea
Coffee 2.5
ESPRESSO 3
MACCHIATO 3
LATTE 4.5
MOCHA 4
CAPPUCCINO 3
MATCHA 4

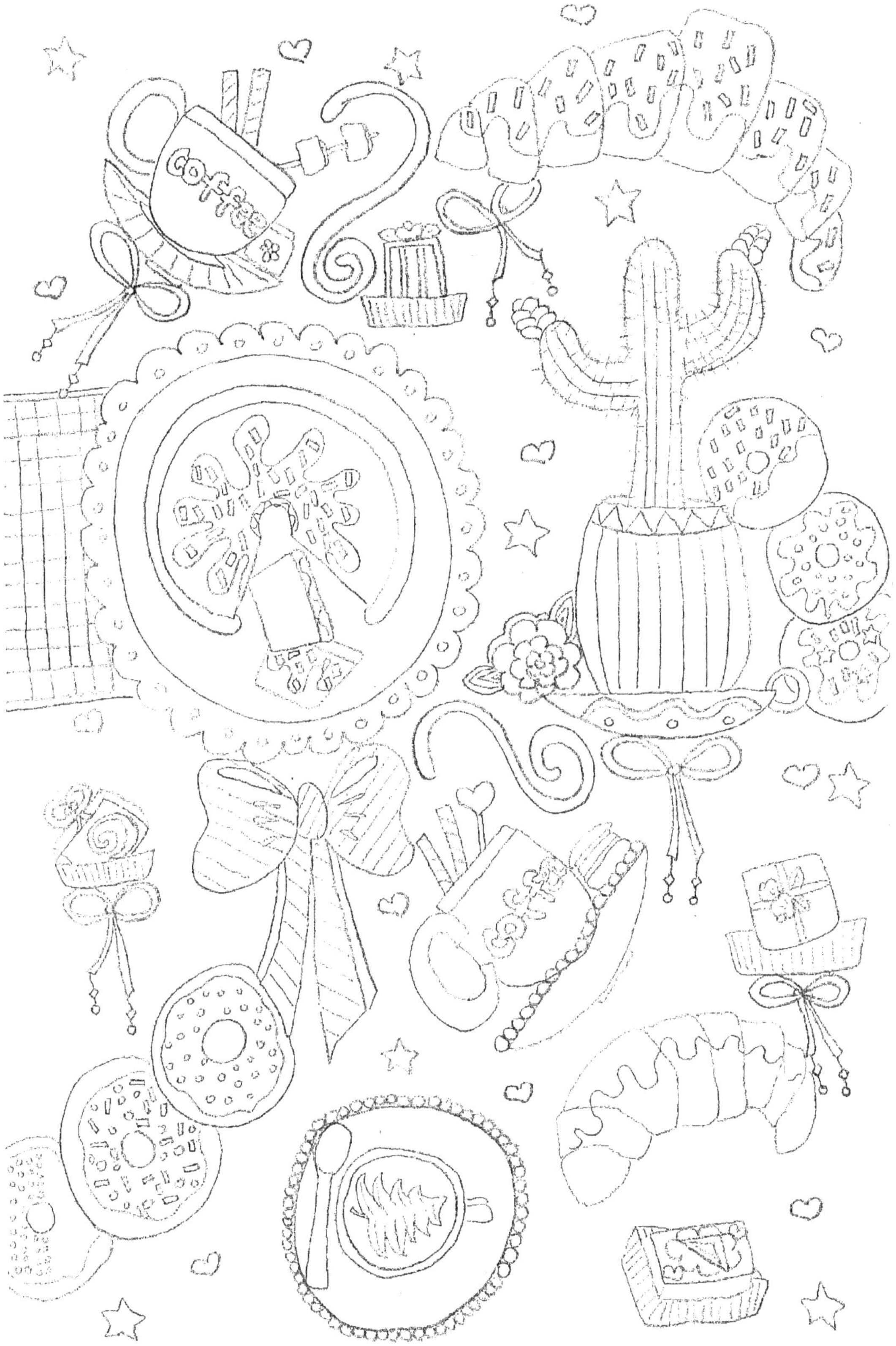
Coffee
Coffee

Coffee
Coffee

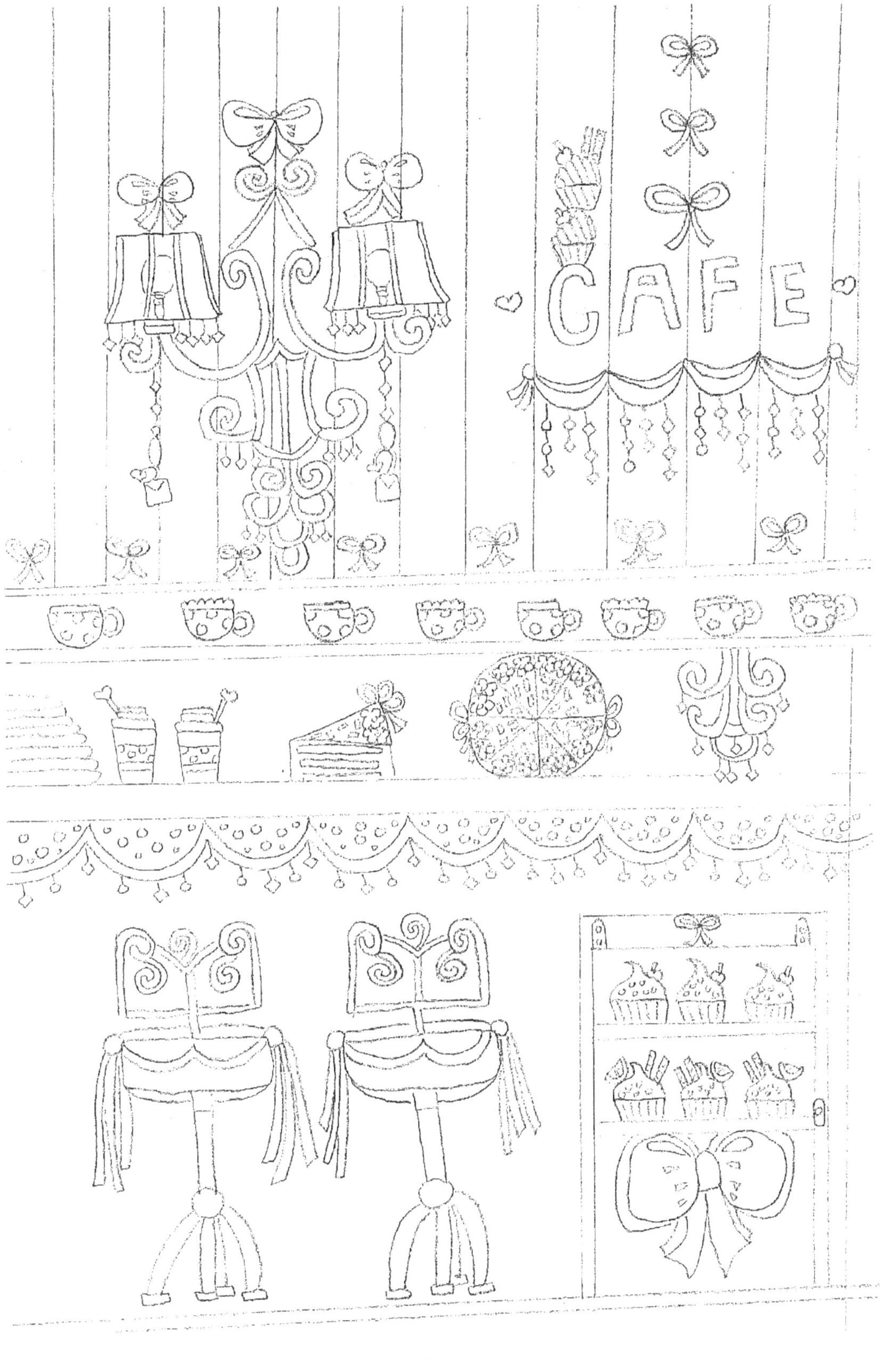
CAFE

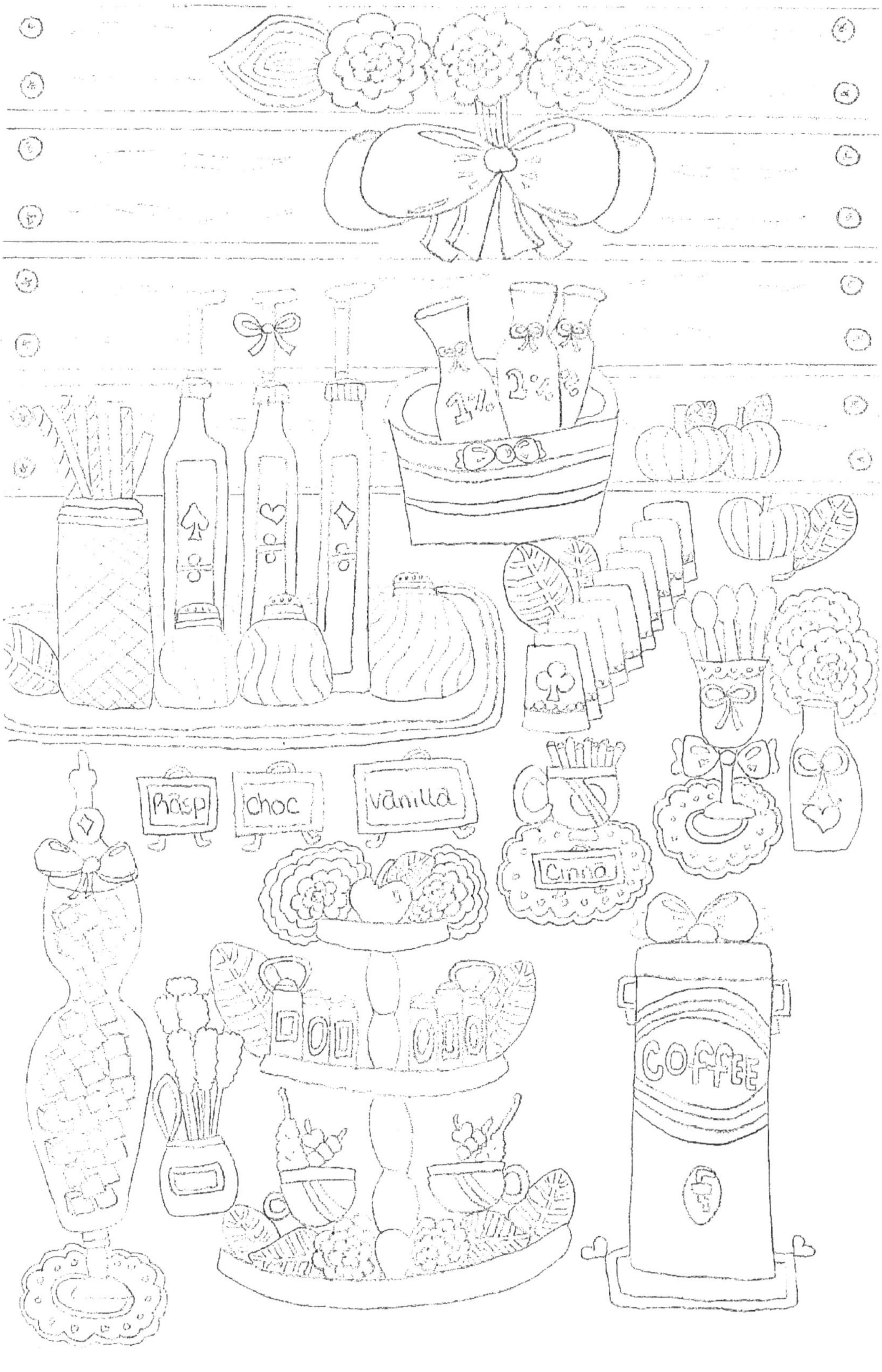

1%
2%
Rasp
choc
vanilla
Cinna
COFFEE

Tea me
CAKE

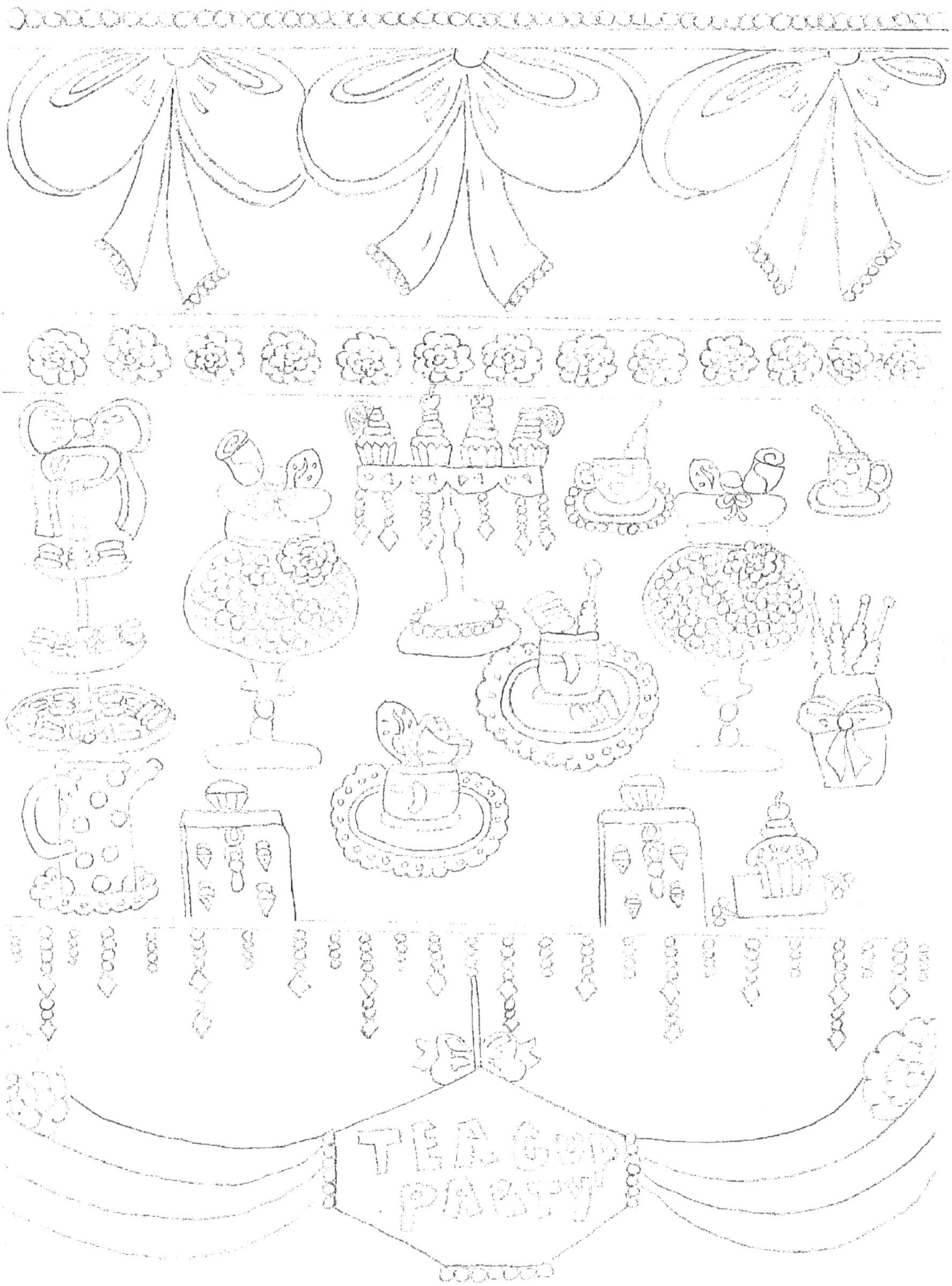
TEA CUP
PARTY

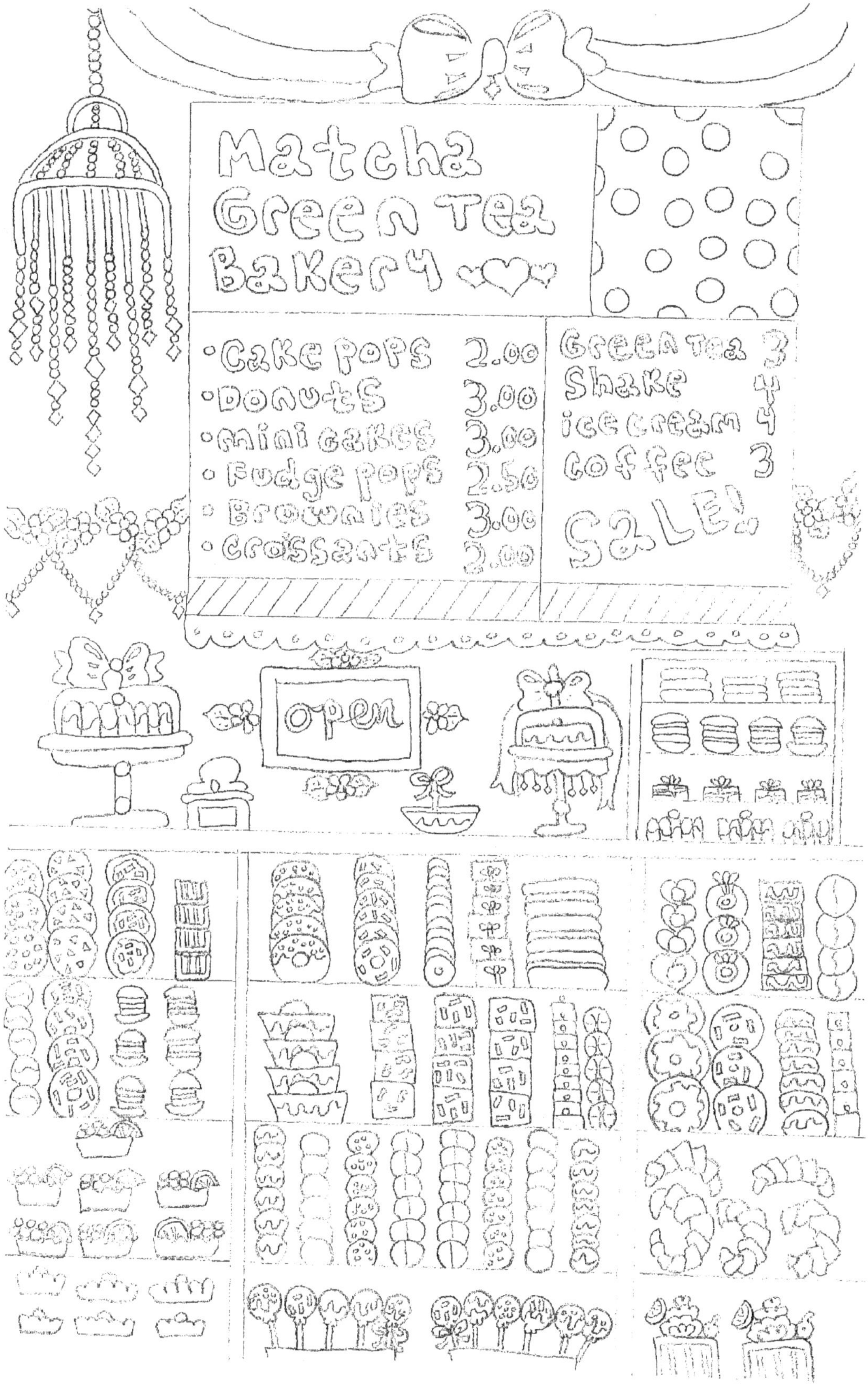
Matcha Green Tea Bakery
Cake pops 2.00
Donuts 3.00
mini cakes 3.00
Fudge pops 2.50
Brownies 3.00
Crossants 2.00
Green Tea Shake 3
4
ice cream 4
coffee 3
SALE!
open

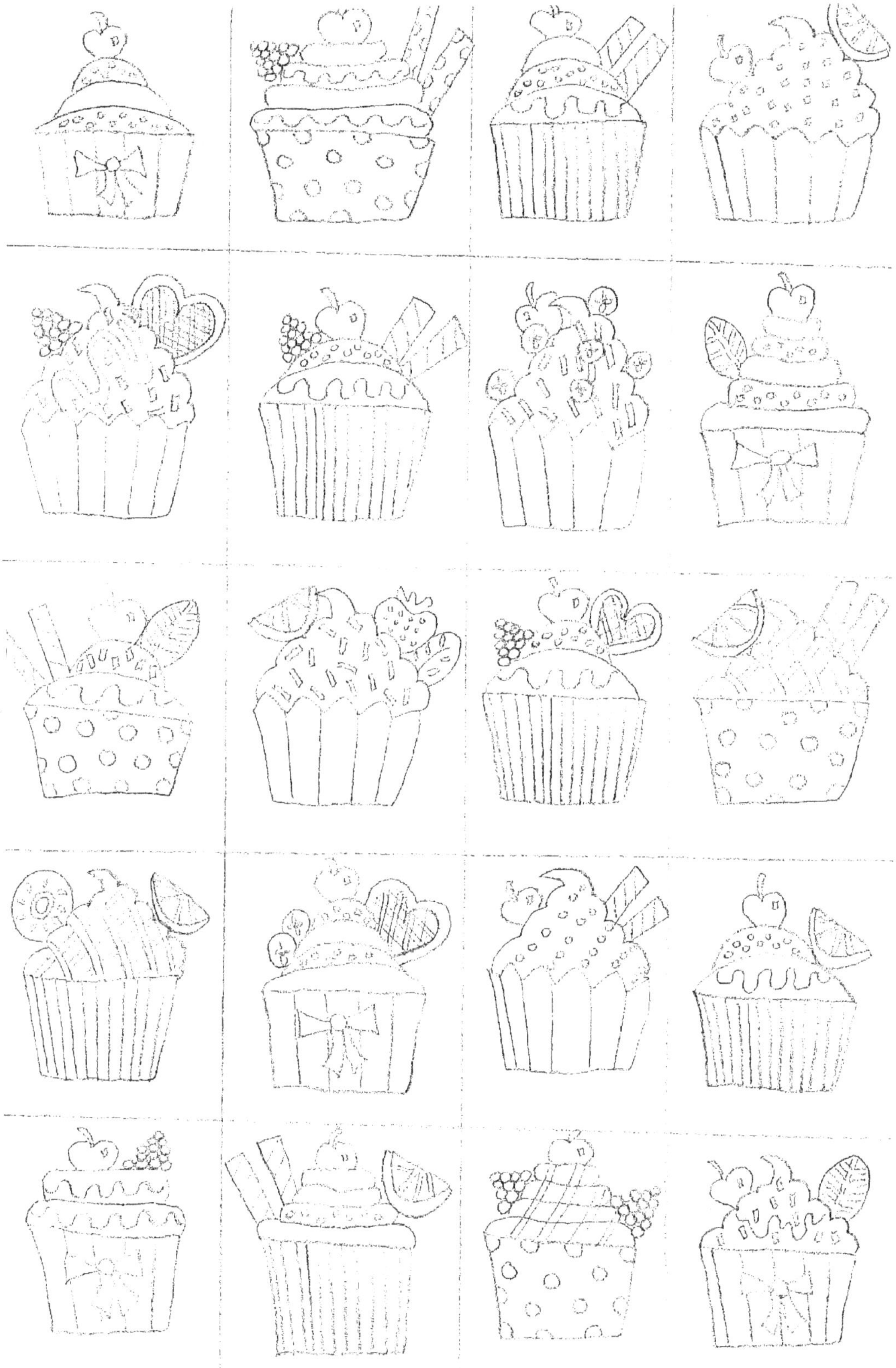

Tea Room
Bakery Sweets

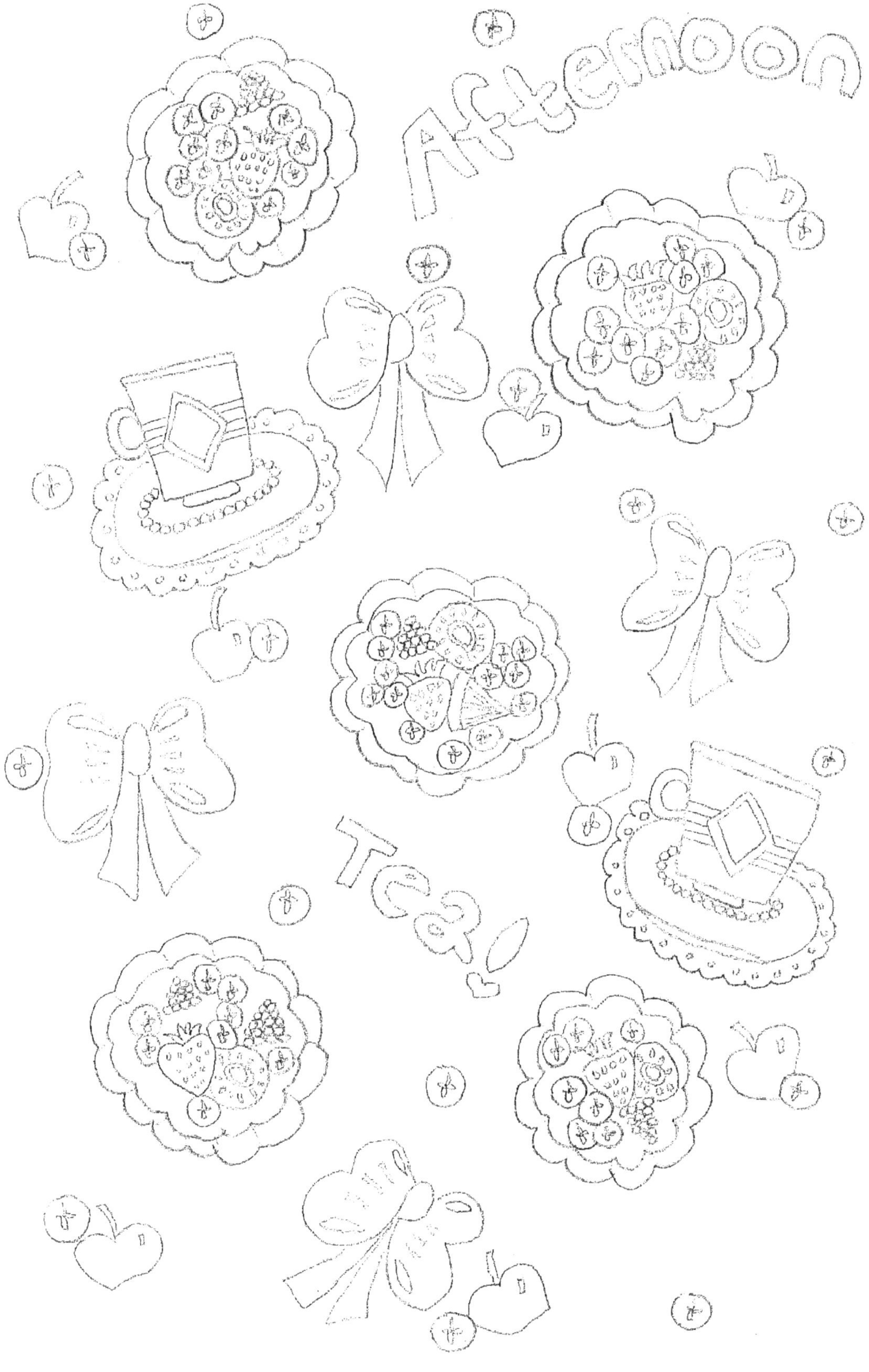
Afternoon
Tea

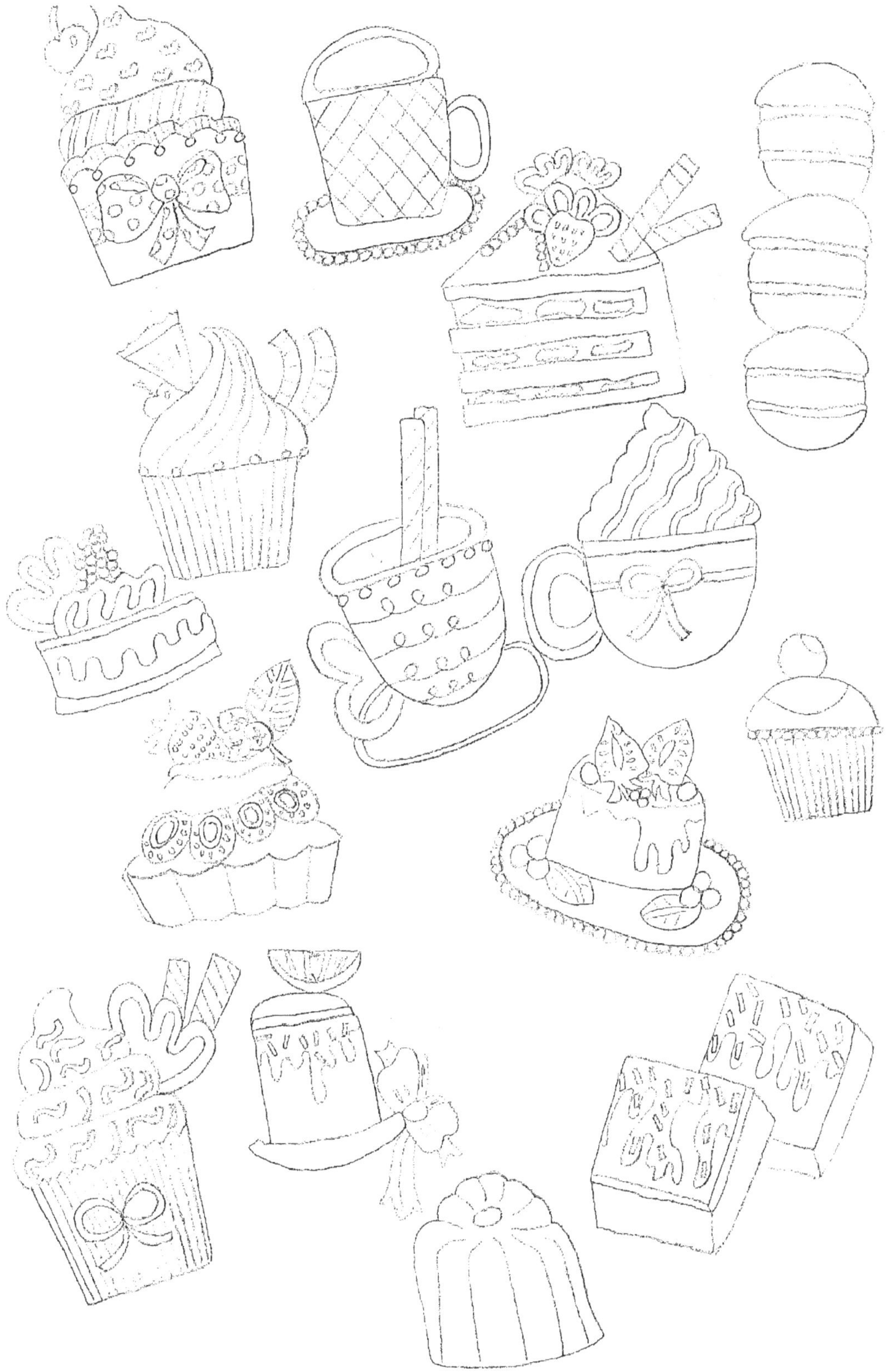

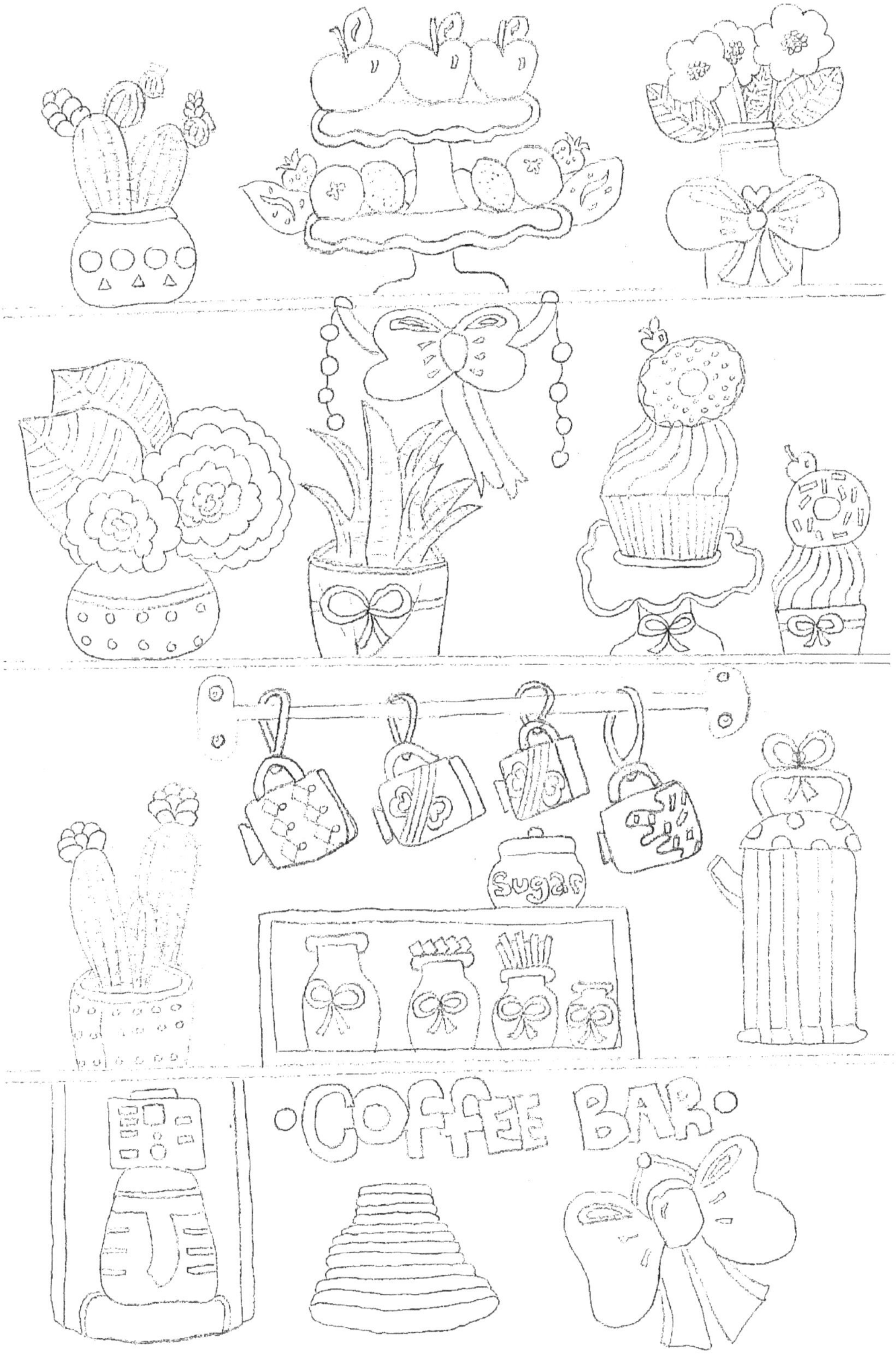
Sugar
COFFEE BAR

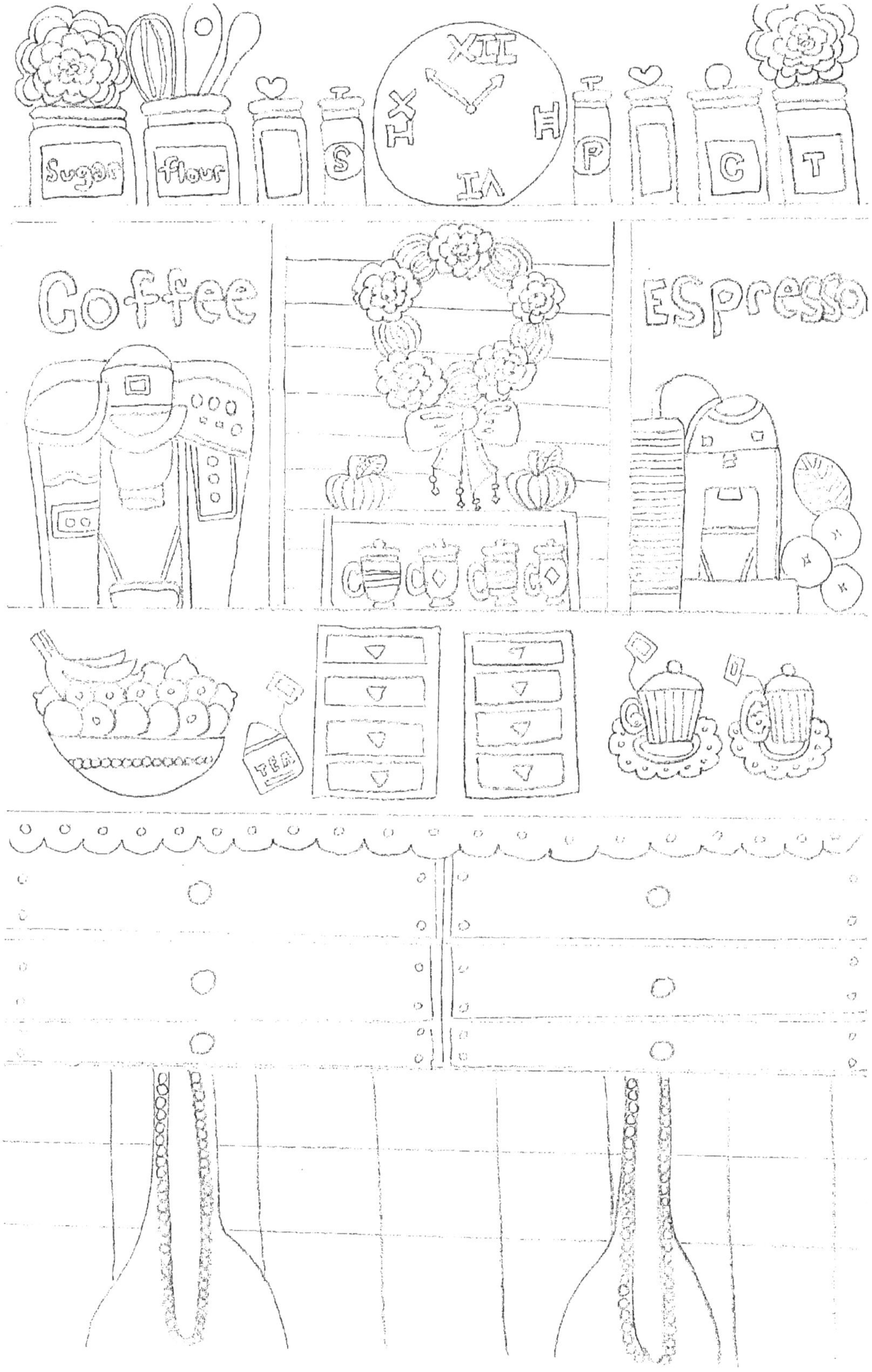
Sugar
flour
S
P
C
T
Coffee
Espresso
TEA

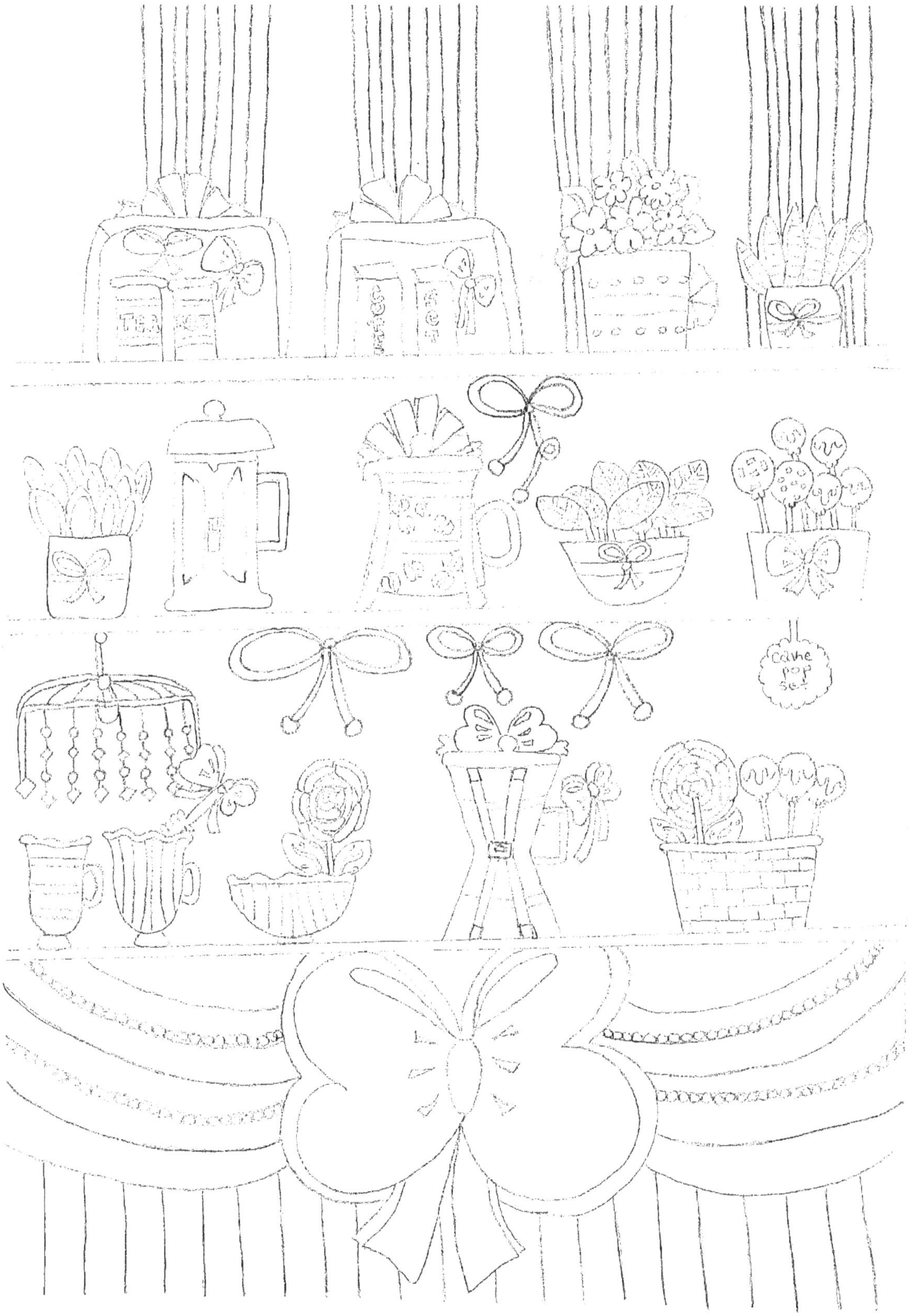
TEA
cake pop set

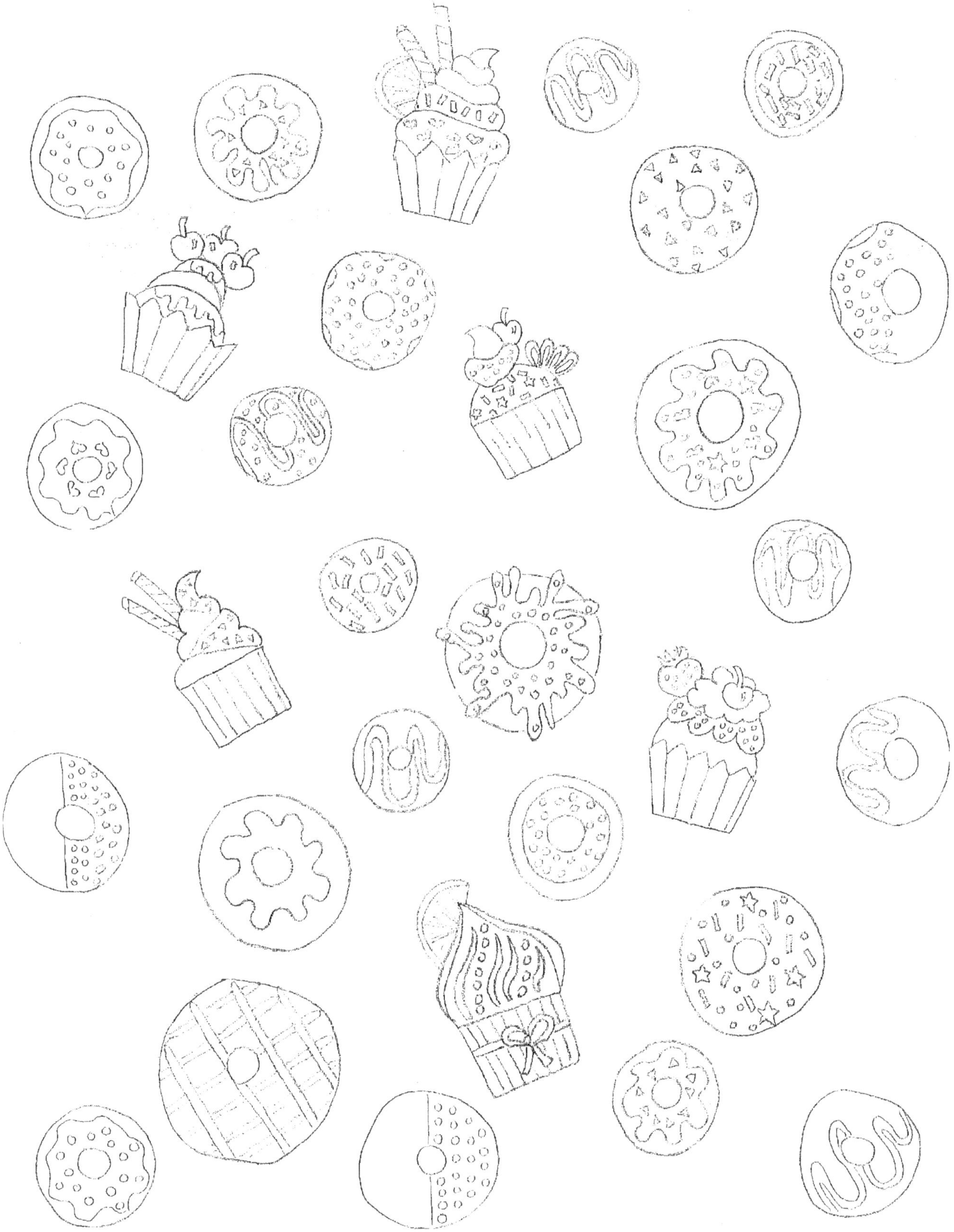

TEA
Coffee
TEA
TEA
TEA

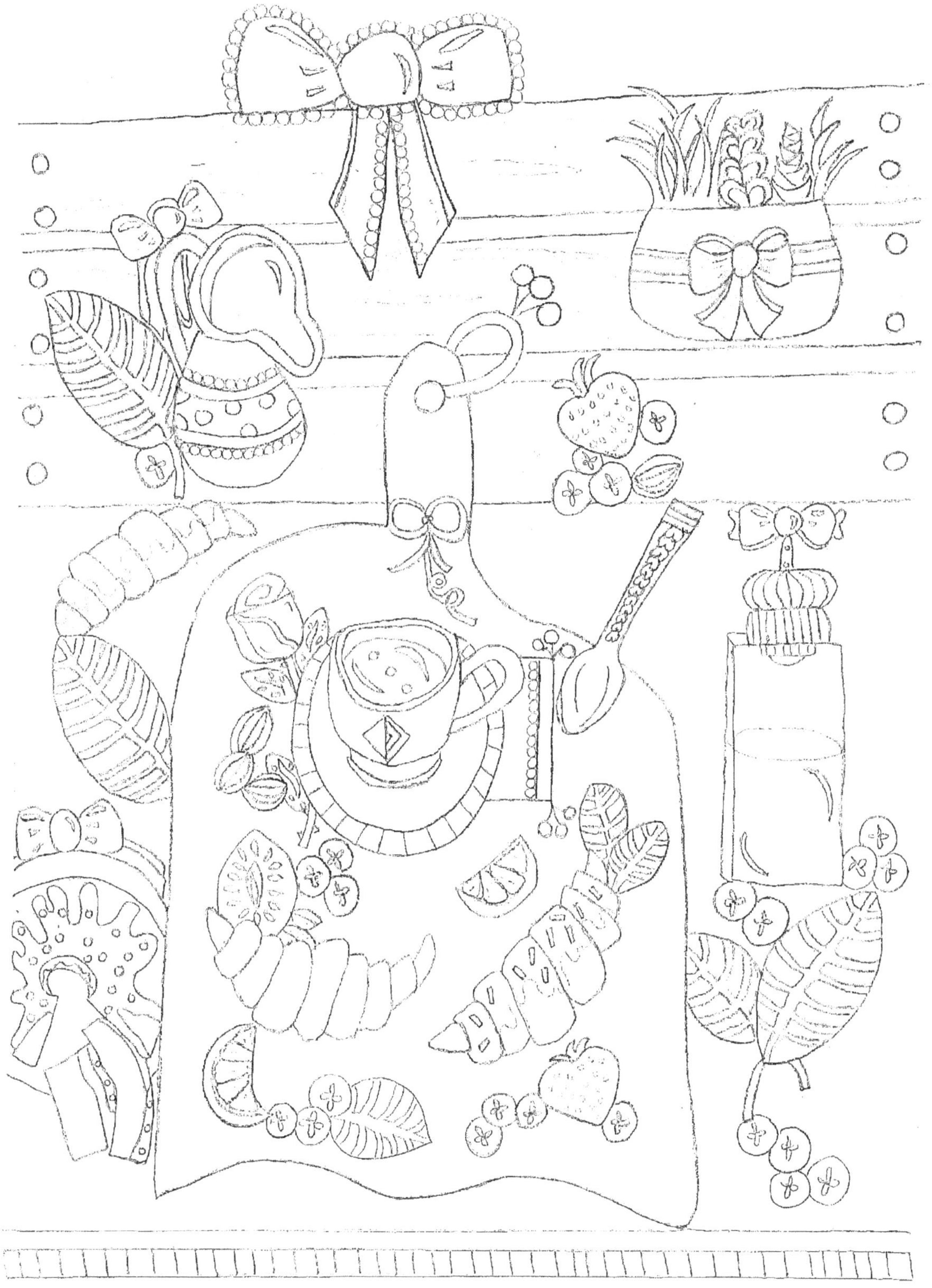

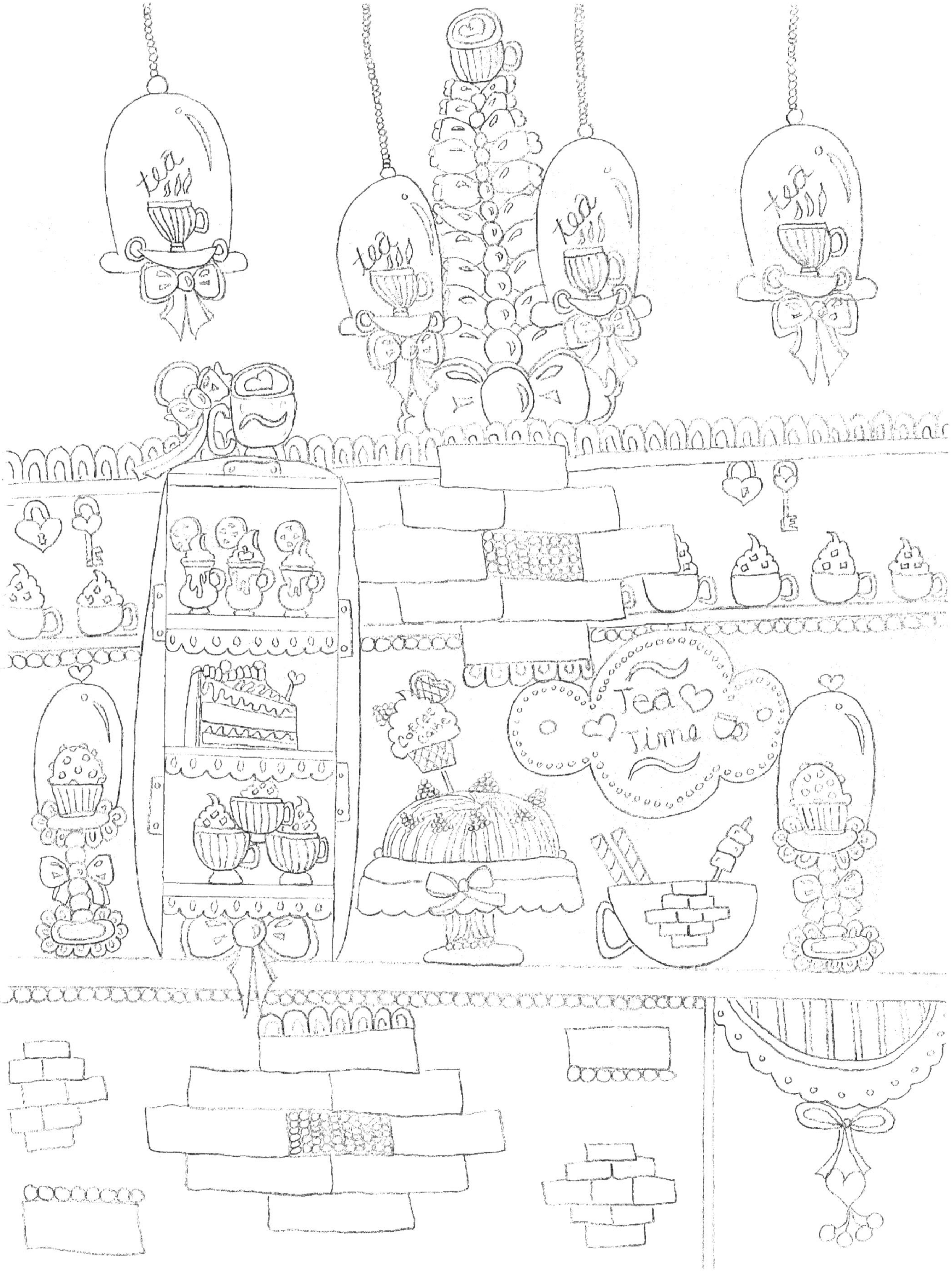
tea
tea
tea
tea
Tea
Time

Green
TEA
~TEA~

Come for tea
left with cake
Tea & Treats
Jelly
Jelly
Welcome
Tea
Hello!

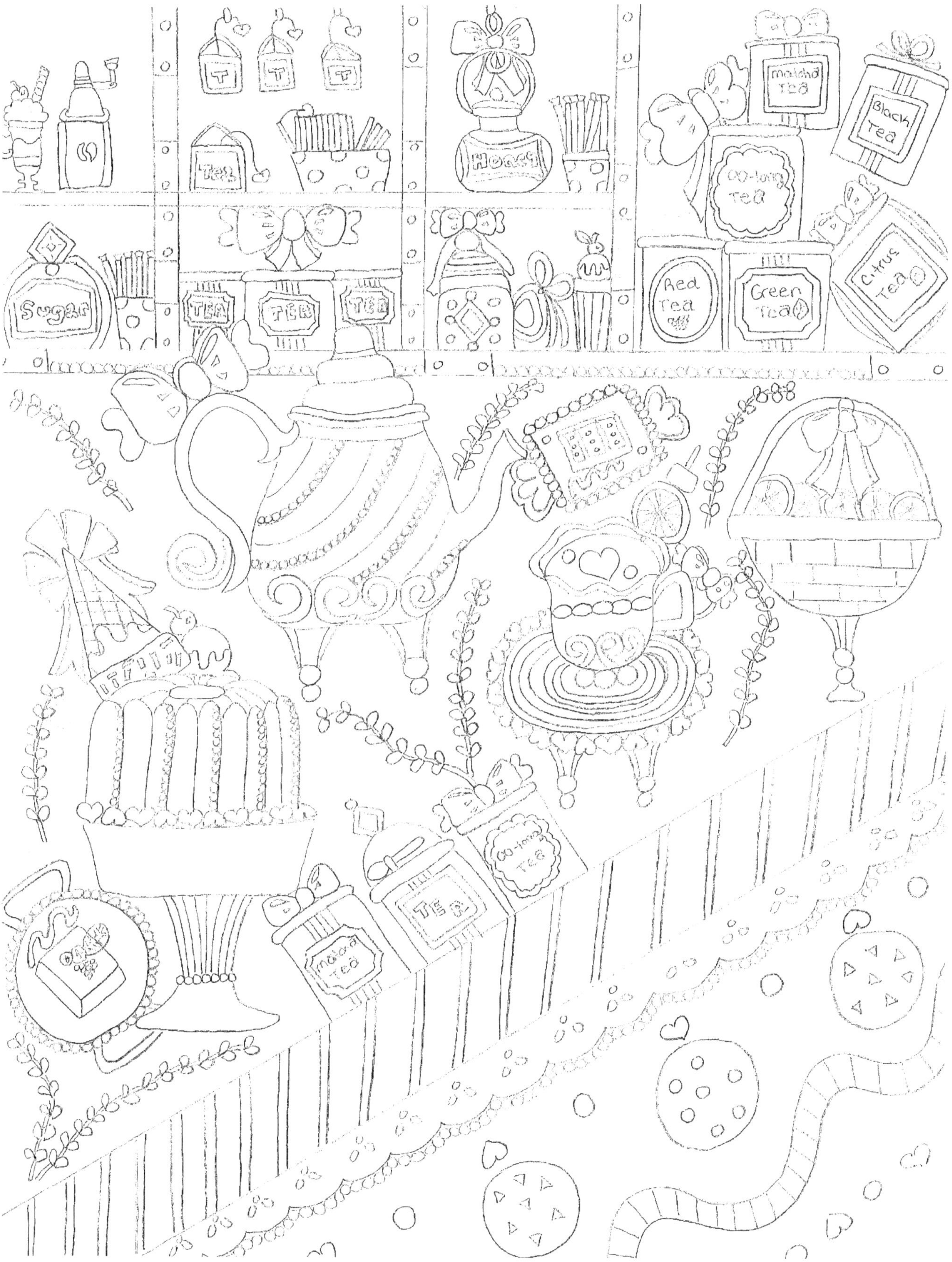
Matcha Tea
Black Tea
Oo-long Tea
Honey
Sugar
TEA
TEA
TEA
Red Tea
Green Tea
Citrus Tea
Oo-long Tea
TEA
Matcha Tea

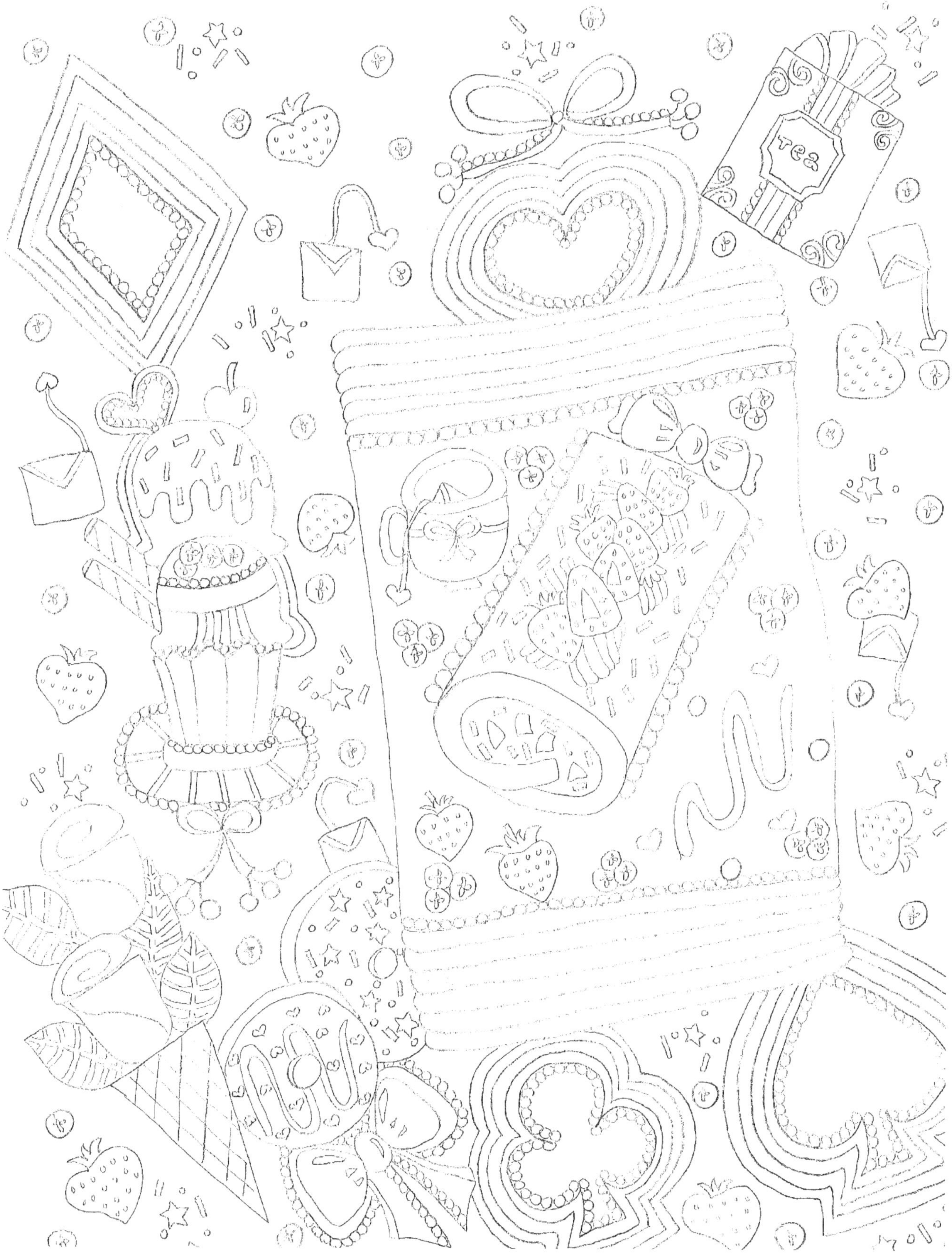
TEA

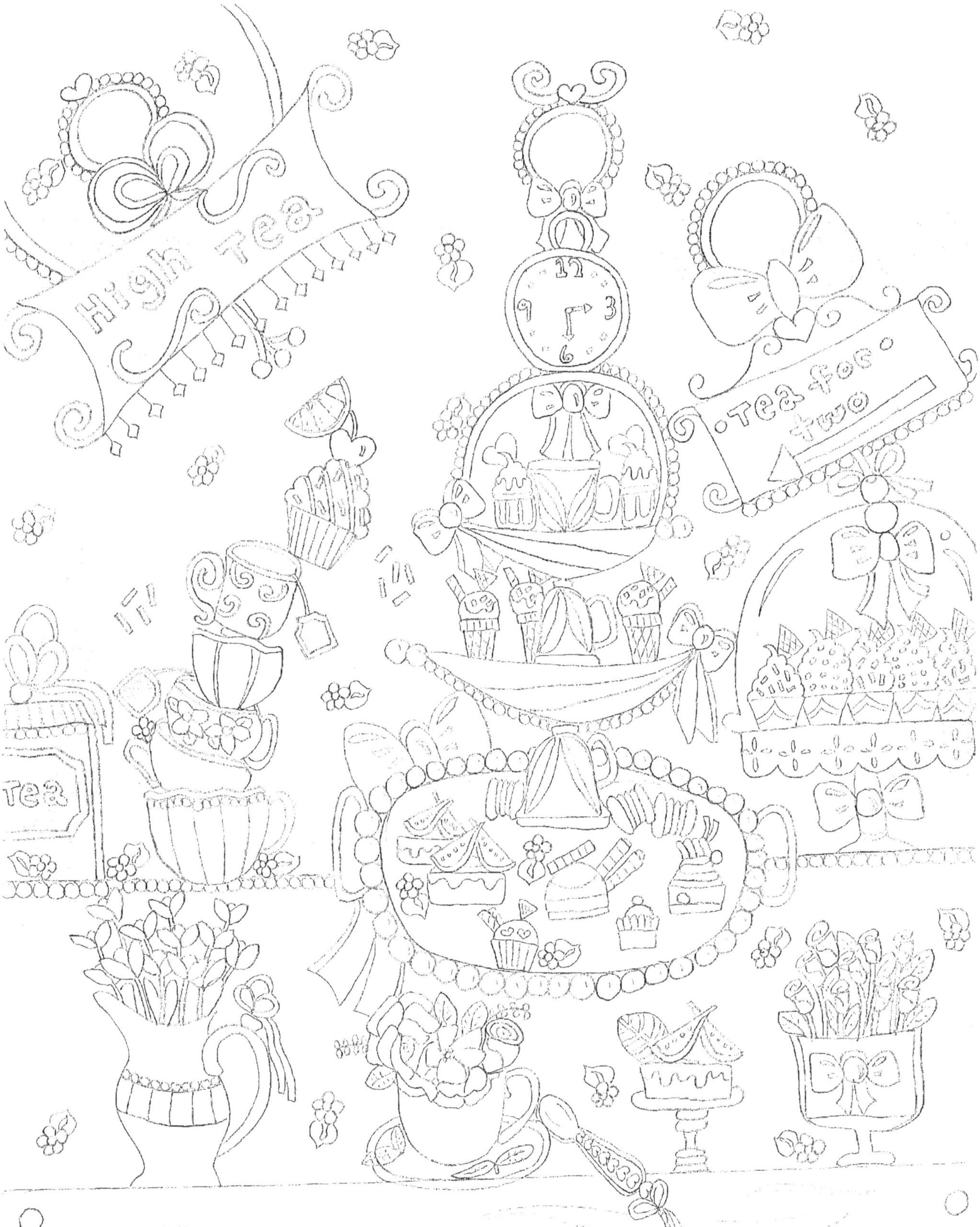
High Tea
Tea for two
Tea

Cake
TEA
TEA
TEA
Apricot Jam
Black-berry Jam
Rasp Jam

hello!
Cakes
fresh oranges
BAKERY
fresh fruit
Cakes
fresh coffee
Cakes
herbal teas
Cakes
TEA
Cakes
Zucchini Bread $4
Donuts

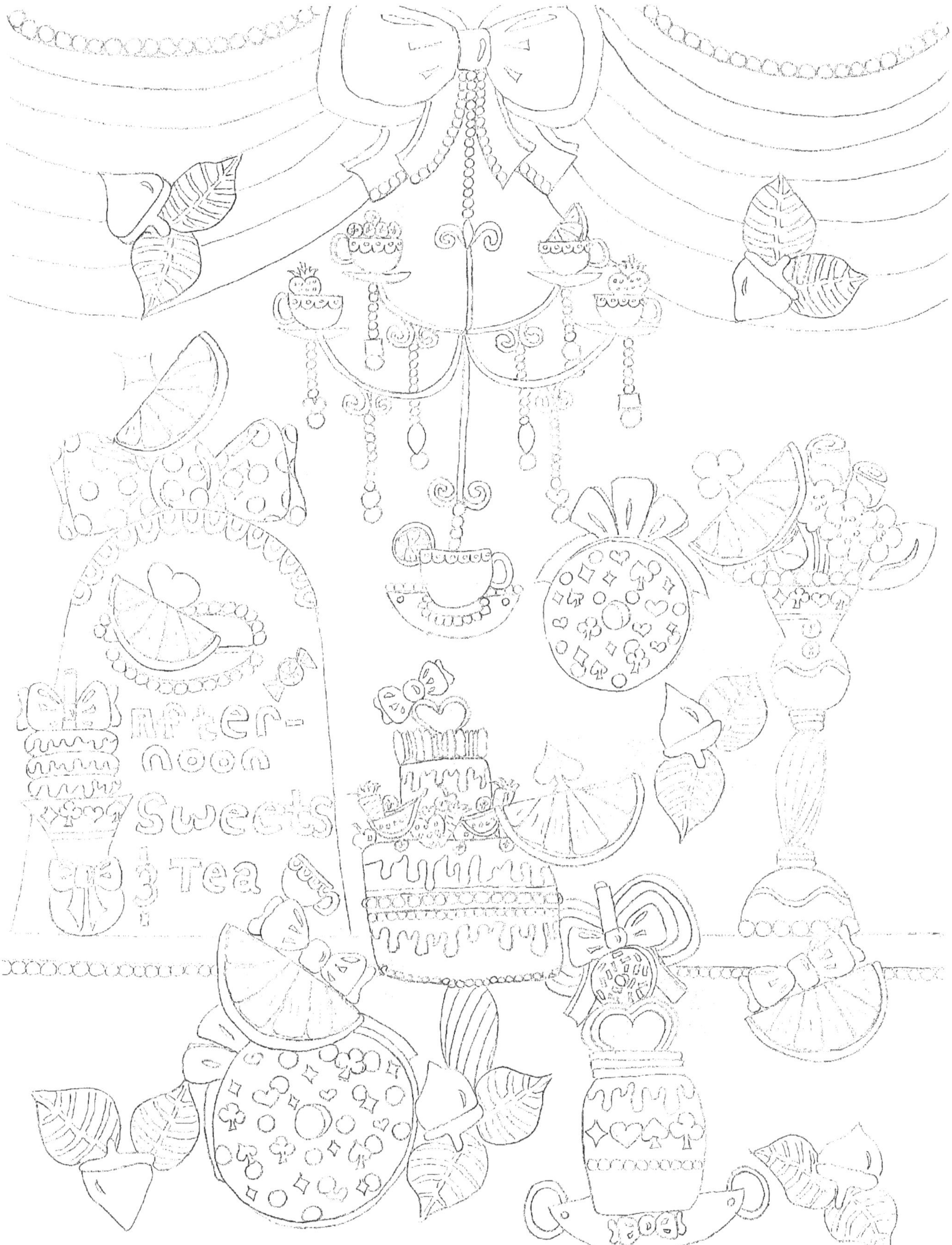
After-
noon
Sweets
&
Tea

Carrot
Cake
Jam

www.ingramcontent.com/pod-product-compliance
Lightning Source LLC
Chambersburg PA
CBHW081739220526
45468CB00008B/2167
9781720737537